EAGLE DOWN

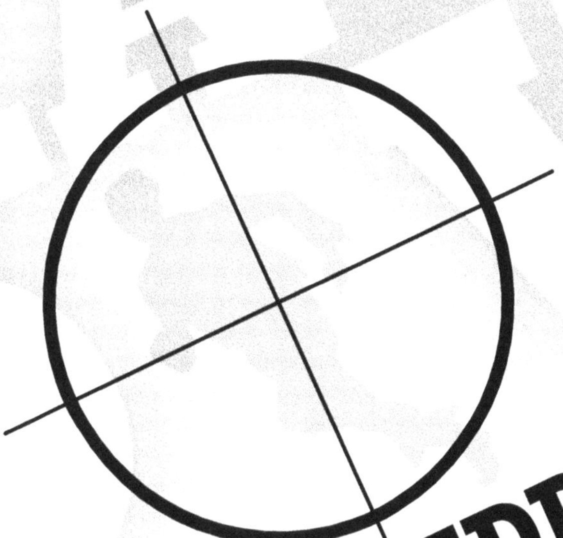

THE UNPRODUCED SCREENPLAY

IB MELCHIOR

Eagle Down: *The Unproduced Screenplay*
© 2012 Ib Melchior. All Rights Reserved.

No part of this book may be reproduced in any form or by any means, electronic, mechanical, digital, photocopying or recording, except for the inclusion in a review, without permission in writing from the publisher.

Published in the USA by:
BearManor Media
PO Box 1129
Duncan, Oklahoma 73534-1129
www.bearmanormedia.com

ISBN 978-1-59393-727-0

Printed in the United States of America.
Book design by Brian Pearce | Red Jacket Press.

INTRODUCTION

It is not unusual for a good book to be turned into a motion picture script, but it is unusual when the opposite happens, yet that is the story of "Eagle Down," which was born as a motion picture screenplay.

Back in the late 1950's there was a court case in Los Angeles of a man who had amnesia, could not even remember his own name, and I was fascinated. I had a very good friend who was a psychoanalyst and discussed the matter with him. I learned of something called amnestic aphasia, that meant the loss of any learned memory, the power of speech and leaving the victim with absolutely no knowledge of his past life — like a new born baby, but with the cunning and reasoning power of an adult — or, in essence, having to function like an animal. In fact, that was the first title of this screenplay, "The Animal."

At that time I had also for the first time visited Death Valley in California, and was struck by the totally hostile, forbidding environment, with the steep, craggy, multi-colored cliffs, the vast stretches of barren sand desert, the jagged, razor-sharp salt pinnacles and poisonous water holes, and I wondered what would happen to a victim of amnestic aphasia should he suddenly find himself stranded in this deadly wilderness, not knowing the fundamental facts, such as you cannot walk on water or when the sun goes down and disappears, will it ever re-appear? How would he survive? And finally, a third bit of interesting information came my way, the experimentation by the Air Force with a special super secret aiming device, and I put the three together and came up with "The Animal."

Unfortunately, the producer who was interested in producing the film passed away, and after attempting to carry on alone, I decided to turn the script into a book, but with a different title. At that time I had a good friend who was the Audience Research Director at MGM, researching the best titles for their films. 15% of all moviegoers go to see a film because of its title, so the title is of importance. I thought I would avail myself of this contention and come up with a good title for my book, and I gave my friend five titles to choose from. "The Animal," "The Chase," "The Marcus Device," from the Air Force research program, "The Seven Inch Wilderness," that wilderness that lies between your ears, and "Eagle Down," from the name of the plane that crashes in Death Valley. The "Marcus Device" won, hands down.

The novel, "The Marcus Device," was published by Harper & Row in 1980. It got glowing reviews — one very observant critic even wrote that the book would make a great motion picture! The script has been optioned several times — but with no result. So why has it not been produced? Perhaps the would-be producers ran into the same unlikely obstacle that bedeviled me: Casting the amnestic victim.

When I wrote the script, it was shortly after I had worked on a film, that was based on one of my own war time experiences, and starred Charles Bronson, whose dialogue director I had been on the film, as well as serving as a special advisor. Bronson, who was very popular in those days, sort of stuck in my mind as a perfect star for my film. He was an accomplished actor whose energy seemed about to explode from him. I showed him the script and he loved it — but, after analyzing the part, he decided against taking it on, not feeling comfortable with the special challenge for the actor who took on the part, to do it justice. The same reaction happened with the next casting possibility, Christopher George, famous for his starring role in the popular TV series, "The Rat Patrol" — with the added plus of casting his real-life wife, Lynda Day George, as his screen wife, their talents, too, could have carried the story. And there were a couple more, all declining the challenge. Nick Adams comes to mind, at the time the up-and-coming young star of the successful TV series, "The Rebel," who tragically later took a fatal overdose of prescription medicine at the age of 36.

Death Valley is still there — and so is my script, still looking for a challenge-proof producer *and* star.

Ib Melchior

"EAGLE DOWN"

FADE IN:

INT. COCKPIT OF F-15 FIGHTER JET - DAY

Tom Darby, mid thirties, handsome, in flying gear, is sitting in the cockpit having just unloaded his missiles. Suddenly, <u>WHAM</u>! The plane has been hit and is on fire, out of control. Tom grabs the D ring between his knees - and pulls.

EXT. JET - Ejection seat shooting from F-15; the parachute deploys.

CLOSE SHOT - TOM - He pulls out his survival radio from his vest.

>   TOM
>   Cardinal Flight. This is Cardinal Three.
>   I'm in my chute and OK.

At once a VOICE crackles over the radio.

>   VOICE
>   Rog. Cardinal Three. This is Cardinal Four.
>   I have you in sight. I see no activity
>   below.

Tom stuffs the radio back into his vest and concentrates on his descent. The rocky desert below is rising fast.

>   SUPER: <u>OPERATION DESERT STORM</u>
>   <u>SOMEWHERE IN IRAQ</u>

EXT. DESERT HILL - DAY

Tom lands roughly. The terrain around him is a typical Iraqi desert, dotted with rocks and sandy hillocks, grown with Tamarisk and other thorn bushes as well as with Rantherium and Papposum shrubs. A craggy rock hill is about a hundred feet away. Tom pulls his chute and struggles out of the harness. He looks up. The SOUND of a plane streaking by overhead is heard. Tom pulls his radio from his vest.

>   TOM
>   Cardinal Four. Cardinal Four. This is
>   Cardinal Three. I'm down.

>   RADIO VOICE
>   Rog, Cardinal Three. Cardinal Flight is
>   Bingo fuel. Keep yourself together, good
>   buddy!

                    TOM
          Rog, Cardinal Four.

He looks up.

POV - An F-15 is flying over the desert hill, and on...

CLOSE SHOT - TOM - He places his radio on the ground next to him; he checks his pistol; he glances toward the radio. It is silent. Suddenly:

                    RADIO
          Cardinal Three, this is Warthog One. Do you
          read?

                    TOM
          Cardinal Three reads you five by. How far
          out are you?

                    RADIO
          About four minutes out. We've got a Saars
          standing by. Need direction.

                    TOM
          Rog.

He flips the switch on his beeper; anxiously he scans the desert and the hillside for signs of trouble.

                    RADIO
          We're coming in. Give us another hold down.

Again Tom flips the switch. The SOUND of approaching planes is heard. Tom looks up expectantly.

POV - Two A-10's are streaking toward the desert hill.

                    RADIO
          Cardinal Three, we're going to put some
          Willie Pete in to mark the way.

                    TOM
          Rog, Warthog.

The PLANES pass over the desert hill and fire white phosphorous smoke bombs that hit the ground, sending columns of smoke billowing up to mark the site.

                    RADIO
          Cardinal. We're going out to meet the Saars.
          He'll be here in a few minutes. Sit tight.

They fly off, disappearing over the hill.

CLOSE SHOT - TOM - He is watching tensely. Presently the distinctive WHOP, WHOP, WHOP, WHOP SOUND of the big rescue chopper is heard. Tom looks eagerly in the direction of the sound. The big Saars chopper is approaching over the hill.

>   RADIO
> Cardinal Three. This is Saars. We're coming in pretty good. We know where you are. Pop a red smoke.

>   TOM
> Rog, Saars. Red smoke.

Quickly he pulls the end of one of his smoke flares and tosses it a few feet away from him. A plume of dense, orange smoke billows up.

>   RADIO
> We've got your smoke. We're coming in.

SHOT - CHOPPER - The big chopper comes in, low over the edge of the hill heading for Tom. Suddenly small arms fire erupts from the rocks. Puffs of smoke appear among the brush - and the rescue helicopter banks sharply.

>   TOM
> No! Damn it! No!

The chopper pulls up with a roar of power, pursued by the small arms fire.

CLOSE ON TOM - crouched in the desert brush watching the chopper veer off.

>   RADIO
> Shit! The towelhead bastards are playing games again. Got to get out.

Suddenly there is a burst of machine gun fire from the hill. The VOICE of Warthog One comes over the radio.

>   RADIO
> Cardinal. Warthog. Hold on for a few more minutes. We'll have to soften the bastards up some.

Suddenly a bullet slams into the ground inches from Tom's knee. He starts. Another - and another hits.

>   TOM
>   (he is shouting)
> Warthog! Warthog! I'm under fire. I've got to take cover.

As he is talking, his eyes are flying over the terrain.

                              TOM
                    That big hillock. I'll make for it. The one
                    nearest the Willie Pete.

Bent low, clutching his pistol in one hand, his radio in the
other, he quickly moves off.

ANOTHER ANGLE - Tom is executing a broken-field run toward a
clump of desert brush on a small hillock. He is almost there,
when his foot is caught in a hole and buckles under him. He
crashes to the ground. He manages to hold on to his pistol, but
the radio goes flying into the weeds.

Tom gets up. Desperately he searches for the radio. A bullet
hisses through the brush. Close. Too close. Tom starts. And
suddenly, all around him, is the whispering SOUND of death, as
bullets whiz through the desert shrubs. And the small arms fire
is joined by the chattering of a machine gun. In a crouched run,
Tom heads for the brush covered hillock - limping badly as he
moves toward the cover.

The SOUND of a rocket whooshing through the air is heard,
followed almost instantaneously by an ear-rending explosion.
Another and another, as the Warthogs blast the rocks.

SHOT - HILLOCK - Tom comes crashing into the brush. He at once
takes cover.

VERY CLOSE - TOM - He thinks he sees movement in the grass in
front of him. He fires...Nothing...Suddenly the ground some
twenty feet in front of him erupts in little geysers of sand, as
one of the Warthogs strafe the area. There is a lull in the
enemy firing - but suddenly a figure of a man, his head covered
by a <u>kaffiyeh</u>, rises up on one knee only ten feet away from Tom,
and aims a gun at him. Tom fires - and the man's face disintegrates in a crimson spray. Tom fires again, and there is
movement in the grass as other enemy soldiers retreat...Quickly
Tom reloads his pistol. He checks. It is his last magazine. It
will be only a matter of minutes before the enemy will close in
on him - and take him. Grimly he waits...

ANOTHER ANGLE - Suddenly a powerful whirring SOUND captures his
attention. The chopper is returning, the sound growing louder.
Tom looks up. The Saars is whirling down from above, coming
fast, headed straight for Tom's brush-covered hillock. The
figure of a man is standing in the door; both he and the chopper
gunner are spraying the ground below with machine gun fire. The
chopper comes to within ten/fifteen feet above Tom.

Abruptly the chopper pulls up, banks steeply and comes to a
hovering stop. The man standing in the doorway leaps out and
crashes into the brush - as the chopper pulls up and soars away,
fleeing a hail of enemy fire.

CLOSER ANGLE - HILLOCK - The man comes running from the brush. It is Paul Jarman, rugged, mid thirties. Quickly he shrugs a couple of M-16 automatic rifles from his shoulder and throws one to Tom.

                    PAUL
    Try this old cock!

Tom catches the gun. Paul hits the ground next to him.

                    PAUL
    Better'n that popgun you've got.

He fires at some movement among the rocks.

                    PAUL
    The Warthogs'll have the towelheads cleared
    out in a few minutes. You and I can hold the
    fuckers off that long.

Paul fires again.

                    PAUL
    Name's Paul.

                    TOM
    Tom.

They fire, lying side by side in the sand... The enemy fire dies down, and once again the SOUND of the chopper is heard.

                    PAUL
    Here comes the Saars. Ready?

                    TOM
    Let's do it.

They break cover.

WIDER ANGLE - Paul and Tom are zig-zagging toward the chopper just settling down close by. There is renewed, scattered enemy fire. The two men reach the chopper - and rough hands haul them aboard. Tom grins at Paul.

                    TOM
    You saved my ass, pal.

Paul grins back and shrugs. Tom looks out the door. The chopper is churning up the ground, creating billows of DUST...

                                    DISSOLVE TO:

EXT. B-B-Q PIT - SMOKE - DAY

Smoke is rising from some burning hickory chips on a fire.

SUPER: "EDWARDS AIR FORCE BASE"
TWO YEARS LATER

WIDE ANGLE ON POOL - Tom comes on to the pool. He throws the ball to Paul - and dives in. Randi, lithe, late twenties, is dangling her feet in the water. Suddenly two powerful hands grab her from below and dunk her in a splash. Sputtering and laughing, she surfaces; but there is tension in her merriment. Tom is grinning at her.

                      RANDI
    You louse!

                      TOM
    You looked entirely too sybaritic.

He laughs and swims with her to the side of the pool. They climb out and Tom wraps a large towel around her. He starts to pat her.

                      TOM
    Here. Let me help.

Randi gently disengages herself.

                      RANDI
    No thanks. I can dry myself.

                      TOM
    Can I just do the good parts?

Randi looks away - and hands him another towel.

                      RANDI
    I -- I don't think so, Tom.

She turns and starts to walk away. Tom looks after her, concerned.

                                                  DISSOLVE TO:

EXT. DARBY HOME - BASE HOUSING - ESTABLISHING NIGHT

A faint light shines from a rear bedroom window.

INT. DARBY BEDROOM

The lamp on a nightstand is on. CAMERA PANS ACROSS the room, past the uniform jacket of a USAF major draped over a chair, clearly showing the silver wings and the name tag reading: DARBY; past a collection of photographs chronicling the obviously happy life of Tom and Randi together. CAMERA COMES to a brief REST on a night-table on which stands a glass of water and an aspirin bottle, and CONTINUES to a CLOSE SHOT of Randi's bare

                                                      CONTINUED:

CONTINUED:

shoulder and back. She is lying on a bed facing the nightstand. Tom's hand comes into picture and gently touches the smooth-skinned back, which is stiff and unresponding to Tom's exploring touch. CAMERA WIDENS. Randi is lying with her back to Tom, who is clad in pajama pants. He continues to caress his wife, who lies immobile. He bends over and kisses her neck - her ear; she lies quietly, her eyes wide open, facing away from her husband. Tom whisper softly...

      TOM
 Rand?

Randi does not respond. Tom sits back - defeated.

      TOM
 It's all right, honey...It's all right...

But it obviously is not.

CLOSE ON RANDI as she screws her eyes shut, ADJUST TO Tom looking at her with concern...He gets out of bed and walks from the room. CAMERA STAYS WITH Randi; she turns toward Tom; she is about to speak - but can't...From the room beyond the SOUND of a TV set can be heard; a talk show is on...

INT. LIVING ROOM

Tom is trying to concentrate on the TV show...Randi enters the room.

      RANDI
 Tom...Please understand...

Tom looks up in desperation.

      TOM
 I love you, Rand...

      RANDI
 I love you, too...You know that...I just --
 can't help it.

She walks over and sits in the chair opposite him.

      RANDI (Cont'd)
 I don't *feel* like I used to...Everything
 seems -- different now.

      TOM
 It doesn't have to be. We have to live in
 the future - not the past.

                    RANDI
          I don't have anything left...Not after what
          happened.

                    TOM
          It's over. Dammit - it's over! How long do
          you want us to go on like this?...I want you,
          Rand. What do you expect of me?

                    RANDI
          I expect you to understand.

                    TOM
          It's been months.

                    RANDI
          I can't help it...
                    (Suddenly flaring)
          It's not my fault!

                    TOM
          What the hell are you saying, Randi? It's my
          fault?
                    (numbly)
          Let's not argue. We're both tired. Go back
          to bed. I'll be there in a few minutes.

                    RANDI
          Goodnight...

She walks into the bedroom.

                                                            CUT TO:

INT. CORRIDOR

GEN. CLIFFORD RYAN comes walking briskly down the corridor.
CAMERA CARRIES him to a door marked:

               FLIGHT TEST COMMANDER
               Maj. Gen. Clifford Ryan

He opens the door without knocking and enters.

INT. GEN. RYAN'S OFFICE - NIGHT

Ryan enters; Dr. Theodor Marcus, a man in his late sixties, gets
up from a chair.

                    RYAN
          Sorry to have kept you waiting, Marcus.

                    MARCUS
          General Ryan.

                    RYAN
          Sit down.

They both sit.

                    RYAN
          I suppose you can guess why you're here at
          this late hour.

                    MARCUS
          The XM-9?

                    RYAN
          Right. Tomorrow.

                    MARCUS
          Tomorrow!

                    RYAN
          0800. Couldn't notify you sooner. The old
          need-to-know crap.

                    MARCUS
          Even my own baby.

                    RYAN
          We're mounting a test flight of the F-22.
          Iron out some bugs in the latest modifica-
          tions. Classified. Major Darby will be the
          pilot.

                    MARCUS
          Excellent. I know him.

                    RYAN
          He will carry your XM-9. He is totally
          familiar with it, of course. He will employ
          it.

                    MARCUS
               (obviously excited)
          At maximum output? Finally?

                    RYAN
          Yes. We'll need you in the control room.

                    MARCUS
          Of course. Of course.

                                              CUT TO:

INT. CALIBRATION ROOM - DAY

A special chair with a headrest stands in the middle of the room. Tom is sitting in it; two white-uniformed SERGEANTS are with him. They put a bright red helmet on him. It is equipped with a small device held in front of the face-plate by two "arms" protruding from the helmet. On the wall before Tom are fixed several "targets" designated A,B,C, etc. Various photos have been tagged onto them: A picture of an ancient, six-decker-wing plane; a provocative pin-up; a flying saucer, interspersed with up-to-date aircraft. A small umbilical runs from the helmet-mounted device to a computer box standing on the floor next to the chair.

                    SERGEANT
          Okay, Major. You're plugged in. Look at
          target A, please. On your left.

Holding his head steady in the head-rest, Tom shifts his eyes to the target. The sergeants work with the calibration of the device. Paul sticks his head in the door.

                    PAUL
          Don't move!

                    TOM
          Verrrrrrry funny!

                    PAUL
          You're a lucky bastard, you know that?

                    TOM
          Luck? Expertise, my boy. Expertise.

                    PAUL
          Who's flying chase?

                    TOM
          Barnes...Manning himself is flying Chase One.

                    PAUL
              (whistles)
          Hea-vy!

                    TOM
          Guess he wants to see first hand how she
          handles at maximum performance - after the
          new enhancement modifications. After all,
          this generation sight is way beyond what
          we've had before.

                    SERGEANT
          Look at target E, sir. On your right.

Tom does; it is the target with the bikini-clad girl.

                              TOM
          With pleasure.

                                                    CUT TO:

INT. EQUIPMENT ROOM - DAY

Paul is inspecting a seat chute. Tom enters with the sergeant. Tom is wearing the helmet with the eye movement sight mounted on it; the umbilical is hooked to his suit. Tom walks over to Paul; the sergeant goes to a chart and makes a notation on it; Paul is helping Tom into the chute.

                              PAUL
          Got your Buck Rogers eyes all fixed up?

                              TOM
          Calibrated to hit the eye of a mosquito at a
          thousand paces.

Paul is looking at the helmet-mounted device.

                              PAUL
                    (half-serious)
          Never could get over being intimidated by the
          damned thing...You look through it - it reads
          the movements of your eyeballs, and locks
          onto whatever you're looking at - and ADIOS!

                              TOM
          Whoever did coin the phrase: If looks could
          kill?

                              PAUL
          Had to be a woman.

A quick frown flits over Tom's face. Paul gives him a sidelong glance.

                              PAUL
                    (quietly)
          Tom. Is -- is everything okay?

Tom looks up quickly, perhaps too quickly.

                              TOM
          Sure. Why not?...

                              PAUL
          Hey, Tom. You and I been buddies a long
          time. You know what I'm talking about. How
          -- how is everything now with you guys?

Tom's face briefly clouds over.

                              TOM
                    Fine, Paul...Fine.
                              (it's obviously not so)
                    Oh, hell, Paul, nothing's changed. Ever
                    since that damned -- accident I can't seem to
                    reach her...If only I'd been <u>there</u>.

                              PAUL
                    Tom --

The sergeant calls from the door.

                              SERGEANT
                    All set, sir.

Paul slaps Tom on the shoulder.

                                                            CUT TO:

EXT. BUILDING - DAY

Tom comes from the building followed by the others; he walks to a
waiting pickup truck and hops in the back...Paul gives him an
informal "friend-type" salute; Tom responds. The truck drives
off toward the landing field in b.g. Paul looks after the
departing truck. His face grows sober.

                                                            CUT TO:

EXT. FIELD - DAY

The plane taxis into position and takes off...

INT. TEST FLIGHT CONTROL ROOM

There is general activity as technicians and officers prepare to
monitor the test flight. "CONTROL ONE" (LT. COL HARNUM) is
standing with a microphone in his hand.

Following shots are:

     TOM - in the cockpit of the F-22...

     CONTROL ONE and DR. MARCUS in the Test Flight Control
     Room...

     MANNING - in the chase plane, Chase One...

and INTERCUT with SHOTS of the F-22 test plane and the chase
planes, as well as B & W FLASH CUTS as indicated.

                              TOM
                    Control. This is Eagle One. Forty seconds
                    out on XM-9 system wet run.

                        CONTROL ONE
                Roger, Eagle One. We read you.

PLANES IN SKY - The F-22 and two chase planes, all climbing.

                         MANNING
                Tom...This is Chase One. You're looking
                good.
                         (ANGLE ON TOM, listening)
                You've got a real sweetheart there!

A quick frown flits over Tom's face.

QUICK FLASH CUT - RANDI'S FACE - BLACK AND WHITE - As she is seen in opening, disturbed.

                          TOM
                Roger, Chase One.

ANGLE ON F-22, streaking through the sky...

ANGLE ON CHASE PLANES zooming alongside...

DESERT TELEMETRY TOWER - The device is tracking...

TEST FLIGHT CONTROL ROOM - General hum of activity...

CLOSER ANGLE - CONTROL ONE

ANOTHER ANGLE - DR. MARCUS

                      TOM (OVER P.A.)
                Still climbing.

                       CONTROL ONE
                Any signs of stress?

                          TOM
                Negative.

THE PLANES - The F-22 is leveling out; the chase planes can be seen at a little distance.

                       CONTROL ONE
                Eagle One. Looks like you need to come right
                about five degrees. You're drifting a
                little.

                          TOM
                Roger.

                       CONTROL ONE
                Your flight angle is good. You're holding
                about fifty feet left of track at the moment.

                    TOM
          Roger...Correcting.

                    CONTROL ONE
          Helmet umbilical connected, Tom? Lanyards
          okay?

                    TOM
          Okay.

                    CONTROL ONE
          Okay. Thirty seconds to firing.

                    TOM
          Roger. Thirty seconds.

                    CONTROL ONE
          Telemetry switch.

                    TOM
          On.

                    CONTROL ONE
          Calibration switch.

                    TOM
          On.

                    CONTROL ONE
          Pressure - Tank One.

                    TOM
          Pressure -

QUICK FLASH CUT - CLOSE-UP - RANDI (IN B&W). She looks haunted.

                    TOM
          Pressure - Tank One - normal.

                    CONTROL ONE
          Pressure - Tank Two.

                    TOM
          Tank Two - normal.

ANGLE ON F-22 streaking through the sky.

                    CONTROL ONE
          Minus fifteen seconds. Master Arm - maximum
          output.

                    TOM
          On.

ANGLE ON MARCUS listening tensely.

                        CONTROL ONE
                  Laser Enable Switch.

                            TOM
                  On...

                        CONTROL ONE
                  Ready to fire...Minus five...

CLOSE-UP - TOM

                        CONTROL ONE (O.S.)
                  ...four...three...

CLOSE-UP - MARCUS

                        CONTROL ONE (O.S.)
                  ...two...one...

INSERT - TOM'S HAND ON SWITCH

                        CONTROL ONE (O.S.)
                  Fire!

ANGLE ON F-22 - The plane is hurtling through the air; there is a puff of smoke from a small explosion; the plane goes out of control and begins to plunge toward earth.

                          MANNING
                  Tom!...Tom!...Do you read me?

There is no response, only loud STATIC.

ANGLE ON F-22 - The plane is out of control; it goes into a spin or deep dive; it is trailing smoke and debris.

ANGLE ON TOM - The aircraft is spinning down...

                          MANNING
                  Tom! Tom! Punch out! You're coming apart!
                  Get out!...Eject!

ANGLE ON F-22 - The ejection seat with the pilot explodes out of the smoking plane.

EXT. MOUNTAINS - In the far distance an unidentified aircraft crashes; there is a big EXPLOSION and a column of black smoke.

                          MANNING
                  Control. This is Chase One...Dick. Eagle
                  One is down. I repeat - <u>Eagle Down</u>! In the
                  Sierra Foothills. Near Mount Whitney. Chute
                  has some torn panels. I show him 322 at 64
                  off China Lake.

TEST FLIGHT CONTROL ROOM. The P.A. is still on.

                        CONTROL ONE
        Roger. Copy. Chopper's on the way

He picks up a phone. Marcus looks stricken.

                      CONTROL ONE (O.S.)
        Get me security...

                                                  CUT TO:

INT. OFFICE OF COL. JONATHAN HOWELL, COMMANDER, 6517 TEST WING - ESTABLISHING SHOT - DAY

The office is severe and functional. On one wall is a large map of the entire desert area; on others framed pictures of the latest Air Force jets. On the desk, a nameplate reading: COL. JONATHAN HOWELL - COMMANDER 6517 TEST WING. COL. HOWELL - a man in his late forties, authoritative, somewhat brusque, is standing at his desk talking on the telephone. He is at the same time trying to look out the window; in the distance - outside - can be heard the wail of a SIREN.

                            HOWELL
        ...the choppers are already on their way...
        Yes...we know the exact spot...Right...And
        medical -- now...And notify the Inyo National
        Forest Rangers...Right!...I want to be kept
        fully informed.

He hangs up; he stands for a second looking out of the window. The SIREN is dying down. Then he again picks up the phone.

                            HOWELL
             (on the phone)
        Get me Captain Paul Jarman!

                                                  CUT TO:

EXT. POOL AT OFFICERS CLUB - DAY

Randi dives gracefully into the pool. She swims the length of the pool, turns and swims over to a group of young WOMEN sitting at the pool's edge. She is about to make a comment, when one of the other women looks up, past her, with a suddenly sobering face. The others quickly follow her gaze - and fall silent. Randi turns.

CLUBHOUSE DOOR - Paul stands in the door.

ANGLE ON WOMEN as they watch his approach, each apprehensive with her own fears. Paul joins the group. Randi stands up to meet him.

                              RANDI
          Hi, Paul. What're you doing here this time
          of day?
                    (then)
          It's - Tom, isn't it?

Paul nods.

                                                  CUT TO:

EXT. ALABAMA HILL - DAY

In the b.g. tower the Sierra Nevadas and Mount Whitney...An Air
Force helicopter is settling down. Three men get out: Airman
First Class NORBERT WILSON, Maj. QUENTIN WARD, USAF Medical Corp;
and Sgt. FREDDY HAYS, a young black. The men run a short
distance from the chopper, looking around. Ward scans the area
with a pair of field glasses.

PANNING SHOT FROM HIGH GROUND - CAMERA PANS, following the rescue
party below; as it PANS, the white expanse of a parachute comes
into view, lying on the rocks in f.g. CAMERA HOLDS with this
parachute in f.g. and the men below. Suddenly Sgt. Hays spies
the chute; he points; the men start up toward the parachute. It
is partly spread out over the rocks; there is an ominous bulge
under the white silk...Ward, Hays and Wilson come hurrying up;
they look grimly at the hidden bulge; Ward bends down and pulls
the chute away; he reveals the harness and a large boulder...The
three men stare at the rock with a mixture of relief and
surprise. Hays picks up the harness; he looks for and finds
something attached to a riser; he holds it out toward Ward.
Attached to the webbing is a small pouch; it has not been
touched.

                              HAYS
          Look, sir. He can't be hurt. He hasn't
          touched his medical kit.

Wilson points.

                              WILSON
          There's a dirt road over there. The Major
          could've seen it as he came down.

                              WARD
          Let's have a look.

They start off.

ROCKS NEAR NARROW CREVICE - Ward, Hays and Wilson are making
their way through the rocks. Wilson is closest to the crevice
entrance in the b.g.; suddenly he picks up something; he holds it
up.

                              WILSON
          Major Ward! Look at this!

The two men run up to him; he hands the object he found to Ward; it is an Air Force helmet without the face plate, its glossy red surface scratched, the EMG sight broken off.

> HAYS
> It's the Major's all right.

Ward turns over the helmet; the other side is crushed in! He runs his fingers across the inside; when he withdraws them - they are dark with clotted blood.

> WILSON
> Man! Must've been a helluva whack to do that.

> WARD
> He's hurt. We've got to find him. He can't be far away.

Wilson points toward the crevice.

> WILSON
> It was lying over there.

They hurry to the crevice; it is extremely narrow; they can see daylight at the other end. Hays examines the ground.

> HAYS
> Someone's been here...

He starts to squeeze through the crevice.

INTO THE CHASM...The three men are laboriously making their way through the narrow crevice.

THE OTHER SIDE OF THE CREVICE - Ward, Hays and Wilson emerge; they look around. Hays goes off a little distance. CAMERA FOLLOWS as Hays is searching among the shrubs along the cliffside. Ward and Wilson are in the b.g. Hays sees a small cave, hidden by the shrubs; he bends down to peer into the dim interior. He moves closer; suddenly - from the hidden interior - a 'creature' leaps at him---Eyes forced wide, lips drawn back in a snarl and hands clawed in front of him - it is Tom! High on the crown on the left side of his head, dry, caked blood has matted his hair. His flying suit is torn and stained and his face streaked with blood. He looks wild, dangerous - and terror-stricken...Violently, he shoves Hays out of his way, raking long gashes across his cheek in his dash to get past him. The impact sends Hays sprawling on the ground - as Tom takes off among the weird stone formations. Ward and Wilson come running up to the dazed Hays.

> WARD
> Hays! What happened?

He kneels beside the man. Hays touches his bleeding cheek.

                    HAYS
          It was the Major...He jumped me...I've known
          him for three years -- and -- he attacked me!

Suddenly Wilson points.

                    WILSON
          Hey! Look!

POV ANGLE - THE ROCKS - On a big, smooth rock stands a lone figure. It is Tom. He is looking toward the men.

THE SEARCHERS - They begin to wave and shout.

                    WARD/HAYS/WILSON
          Hey! Major Darby! Here -- down here! Wait!
          Tom!...Tom!...! Stay where you are! We're
          coming to help you!...

They start to run toward him.

FULL FIGURE - TOM ON THE ROCK - He stands looking off toward the shouting men; there is fear on his face...

REVERSE - ACROSS TOM TO RESCUERS coming toward him in a run. Tom stands still; the three men are still calling to him, as they run toward him. Suddenly he whirls about, jumps off the rock, and quickly flees among the weird stone formations. CAMERA FOLLOWS him as he runs away until he disappears from sight. Ward, Hays and Wilson come running onto the scene; they look around - bewildered.

                    HAYS
          Why! Why is the Major running away!

                    WARD
              (shaking his head)
          I don't know...I just don't know...

Suddenly, far in the b.g., Tom comes into view, jumping from one rock to another.

                    WILSON
          There he goes!

At once they take off in pursuit.

THE ROCKS - Tom is leaping over the rocks; he looks back to where the voices calling to him can be faintly HEARD; uncomprehending, he touches the wound on his head; he turns and clambers up a slope.

ANOTHER ANGLE - THE ROCKS - Climbing across a saddle in the rock formations, Ward, Hays and Wilson are still in pursuit - CAMERA FOLLOWS, as they disappear behind a rock formation.

RESUME TOM as he comes to a flat, boulder-strewn plateau; at once he begins a loping gait out across the area.

CREST OF THE SLOPE - Hays is the first to reach the plateau.

HAYS
There he is!

Ward and Wilson climb up behind him; they set out in pursuit.

THE PLATEAU - Tom is fleeing. He stops; he has come to a long, deep ravine - 12 to 15 feet across. He looks down.

RAVINE - TOM'S POV - The chasm is deep, the sides are virtually perpendicular.

THE PLATEAU - Tom runs a little away along the ravine, first one way, then the other. There is no way to cross; he is trapped. He whirls to face the oncoming pursuers.

ANGLE - TOM AND HIS PURSUERS - In growing panic, Tom backs away from his pursuers - toward the deep crevice in back of him. Ward speaks to him soothingly, as he and his men slowly move in on him.

WARD
Easy, Tom, easy...Don't be afraid...We are your friends...We want to help...Tom -- listen to me...Easy...Easy...Just -- stay where you are...Easy...

Wild-eyed, Tom glances from side to side, desperately seeking a way out; he looks back at his tormentors, then quickly into the abyss gaping in back of him - back to his would-be rescuers - almost upon him...Another few feet...Suddenly he gets a look of desperate determination, with a burst of action, he takes a little run - and leaps over the gaping chasm for the other edge far away...He barely makes it - hanging with his arms over the rim - slowly slipping down, his legs searching for a footing, his fingers digging into the rock...Slowly, he pulls himself up. He glances back across the ravine at the three men.

THE MEN. They stand staring at Tom.

WILSON
Man! Did you see that? He jumped that ravine like -- like a big cat...

HAYS
He could have killed himself. Easy.

ANOTHER ANGLE - On the far rim, Tom gets up. Without a glance back, he trots off - disappearing among the rocks.

> WILSON
> I wouldn't have believed it -- if I hadn't seen it...No, sir. It -- it couldn't be done...

Thoughtfully he stares after the disappearing Tom.

CUT TO:

EXT. EDWARDS AIR FORCE BASE - DAY

MAIN BUILDING, ESTABLISHING SHOT - across sign which reads:

> AIR FORCE FLIGHT TEST CENTER
> Edwards Air Force Base

Air Force personnel can be seen entering and leaving the building.

INT. CORRIDOR

An AIRMAN (female) comes walking down the corridor. CAMERA FOLLOWS her to a door; a sign on it reads:

> MESSAGE CENTER
> CODE ROOM
> Authorized Personnel Only

The Airman enters the room - CAMERA with her...Several AIRMEN and NON-COMS are active in the room. CAMERA MOVES to a CLOSE SHOT of a teletype machine; the machine suddenly starts to clatter away, as a message begins to come in on it. An OPERATOR goes to it first and starts to read:

> PERSONAL FROM CHIEF OF STAFF TO
> COMMANDER AIR FORCE FLIGHT TEST
> CENTER EDWARDS AFB
> URGENT   URGENT   URGENT
> MAJOR DARBY F-22 CRASH EXTREMELY
> REPEAT EXTREMELY SENSITIVE DUE TO
> XM-9 TESTS. IMPERATIVE

> OPERATOR
> Hey, Sergeant! Take a look at this.

The sergeant walks over and reads the message; he reaches for a telephone.

> SERGEANT
> Get me General Ryan's office...

CUT TO:

EXT. AFB HANGAR - WIDE SHOT - DAY

A small group of Air Force officers and non-coms stand at a jet parked just outside the hangar; among them is General Clifford Ryan. The telephone in the General's car, parked nearby RINGS; an officer standing by the car answers; he hurries over to the group; he addresses General Ryan; the General at once follows him to the car - which takes off...

                                                    CUT TO:

INT. GENERAL RYAN'S OFFICE - DAY

Lt. Col. Harnum, Dr. Theodor Marcus, Col. Howell and Gen. Ryan are standing by a large desk. Ryan is reading the teletype aloud:

                    RYAN
          Imperative ascertain cause of accident at
          once. Use appropriate procedures. Project
          vital repeat vital to national defense. Keep
          advising...Warfield, General, USAF, Chief of
          Staff...

Ryan looks from one to the other of the men standing before him.

                    RYAN
          Have you any idea what went wrong up there,
          Colonel Harnum?

                    HARNUM
          It happened the instant the XM-9 was fired.
          It may have been the laser activator. Or a
          pressure tank.

                    RYAN
          Can we rule out sabotage?

                    HARNUM
          Sir. At the moment we can rule out nothing.

Ryan turns to Marcus.

                    RYAN
          Doctor Marcus?

                    MARCUS
          I should be able to come up with some answers
          once I get the XM-9 mechanism from the
          wreckage. It is absolutely imperative that I
          debrief Major Darby as quickly as possible.

Ryan looks at Howell.

                    RYAN
          John? Where do we stand?

                    HOWELL
          The plane pretty much disintegrated. The
          wreckage is scattered all through the moun-
          tains. The Combat Mobility Forces haven't
          yet located any main impact area. As soon as
          they do we'll cordon it off with security
          police. There are hikers and climbers all
          through the crash area.
                    (Ryan nods)
          As for the rescue operation, they have had -
          eh - trouble getting Major Darby.

Ryan nods; he turns to the other two men.

                    RYAN
          That will be all.

When Harnum and Marcus have left, Ryan turns on Howell.

                    RYAN
          What the hell *is* going on out there?

                    HOWELL
          It seems Darby is -- evading, actively
          evading the rescue team. And he's injured.
          We don't know how seriously...

On Ryan, frowning at the message in his hand.

                                                  SMASH TO:

INT. HOWELL'S OFFICE - NIGHT

Howell's fist slams down hard. Major Ward and Paul stand before
him. Howell gets up.

                    HOWELL
          Damn his hide! Walking away from his chute.

                    WARD
          He is not responsible, sir.

                    HOWELL
          Explain that!

                    WARD
          The head injury. Of course, without an
          examination, I --

                    HOWELL
          I don't want a medical diagnosis, Major.
          Just an explanation.

WARD
His brain may be affected. Damaged. He is not himself.

HOWELL
Are you telling me that Major Darby has lost his mind?

WARD
I am saying that I believe him to have suffered brain injury, Colonel. He may be mentally deranged. It's the only explanation for his aberrant behavior.

HOWELL
We'll have to get to him. Fast. As fast as possible. Captain Jarman. I want you to take command.

PAUL
Yes, sir.

HOWELL
I know of your ties to Major Darby. You will be in charge of the operations in the field.

PAUL
Yes, sir.

HOWELL
Major Ward. The medical responsibilities will be yours.

WARD
Of course, sir.

PAUL
We'll start for the area at 0400 tomorrow. That'll put us at first light.

HOWELL
Paul. Apart from all humanitarian reasons, we _must_ find Tom - and bring him back.
                    (picks up a paper)
The report from the crash investigation team states that the plane is a total loss. The telemetering transmissions were cut off completely during the critical period. Tom is the only man alive who knows what went wrong. We've got to know -- or we can start from scratch.

PAUL
I'll organize a maximum effort, the emergency service teams -- and...

                    HOWELL
          You will organize a classified operation. I
          don't want to alert every Tom, Dick and Ivan
          to the fact that we have a deranged test
          pilot with his head crammed full of top
          secret information running loose...

                    PAUL
          I understand.

The telephone RINGS; Howell answers it.

                    HOWELL
          Howell...Yes...Where?...I see...Yes, get a
          complete report...Right.
                    (hangs up)
          Well, your job's just been made easier for
          you.
                    (goes to the wall map)
          That was a report from Inyo. Tom has been
          seen -- halfway up the highest mountain in
          the continental states...

                    PAUL
          Mount Whitney!..
                    (knowingly)
          Taking to the high ground...Like a wounded
          animal...

                                                   CUT TO:

EXT. BAGHDAD ESTABLISHING SHOTS (STOCK) - DAY

Exotic streets scenes with bazaar and shops and a minaret sky
line.

EXT. BAGHDAD - LARGE OFFICE BUILDING - ESTABLISHING

INT. OFFICE BUILDING - ESTABLISHING

Arabs in a conglomeration of dress, military uniforms, western
clothes and Islam garments, go about their business.

INT. OFFICE OF COLONEL GERHARDT SCHARFF - CLOSE SHOT - FRAMED
PHOTOGRAPH WALL

It is a photo of a young SS officer in full SS uniform. As
CAMERA WIDENS AND PANS, we see a man sitting behind a desk
talking on the phone; it is obviously the same SS officer - 46
years later; in front of him is a name plate that reads: COL.
GERHARDT SCHARFF. The office is furnished in a mixture of
Teutonic Western and Mid-Eastern styles. On the walls are photos
of high-ranking Nazis such as Adolf Hitler and prominent Iraqi
personalities including SADDAM HUSSEIN. CAMERA MOVES TO SCHARFF.

                    SCHARFF
          The President has been pleased to find me
          useful in the past...Yes, _Cedi_, a unique
          opportunity...I agree, _Cedi_. That is pre-
          cisely why I brought it to your personal
          attention as Minister of Armament...Yes, the
          device is top secret. It has been extremely
          well guarded. Penetration has been impossi-
          ble. So far...I agree, _Cedi_, the risk should
          be minimal...Of course. I shall personally
          take charge.

He hangs up. For a brief moment he sits motionless - then with
an impulsive gesture of triumph, he slaps his desk.

                    SCHARFF
          Donnerwetter!

He flips on intercom button.

                    VOICE
          Yes, sir.

                    SCHARFF
          Get in here, Richter.

                    VOICE
          Yes, sir.

Scharff get up; he begins to pace. Almost at once the door to an
adjoining office opens and a younger man, RICHTER, enters.
Scharff turns to him.

                    SCHARFF
          Ah, Richter. I shall need some information.
          Quickly. Whatever you can find in our files
          on a Doctor Theodor Marcus.

                    RICHTER
          Yes, sir. Doctor Theodor Marcus.

                    SCHARFF
          Marcus was one of the Werner von Braun's
          associates. In the development of the V-2
          rocket...Get me everything you can on him.

                    RICHTER
          Yes, sir.

He turns to go. Scharff stops him.

                    SCHARFF
          And Richter. For my eyes only.

Richter leaves. Scharff picks up the phone.

                    SCHARFF
          Get me Major Nizar Kahlil.
                    (waits)
          Abu-Ali! Scharff here. This is top prior-
          ity...Have we any agents with technological
          knowledge in Southern California?...I need it
          at once...I'll wait...

He drums his fingers on the desk impatiently as he waits.

                    SCHARFF
          Yes...I see...Two...Is the control still
          located in Los Angeles?...Good. Contact him.
          Orders will be transmitted to him within the
          hour. Tell him to contact the agents.
          Activate them both!

                                                  CUT TO:

EXT. MOUNTAIN - DAY

The Sierra Nevada mountain range with the snow-covered peak at
Mt. Whitney. It is morning. ADJUST TO REVEAL WHITNEY PORTAL
WATERFALL, where water cascades down the mountainside winding its
way through the trees...A deer is standing at the water's edge,
drinking. Suddenly there is a small SOUND from the thicket. The
deer looks up - watching the thicket intently.

ACROSS DEER TO THICKET - There is a movement in the bushes, and
Tom cautiously steps into the little clearing. He stops short
when he sees the deer. For a little while, the man and the
animal watch each other warily, then the deer returns to its
drinking. Tom quietly creeps down to the water and crouches down
to drink, almost imitating the deer.

MOUNTAIN ROAD - A Scout is halted on the road; Wilson sits behind
the wheel; Hays is in the back; he has a small bandage on his
cheek; Paul - next to Wilson - is looking through a pair of
binoculars.

HIS BINOCULAR POV - Tom and the deer drinking.

BACK TO PAUL - lowering the field glasses.

                    PAUL
          Let's go!

MOUNTAIN - TOM AND THE DEER - both drinking; Tom with his face
submerged in the water. Suddenly - in the distance there is the
ROAR of a motor being gunned. The deer looks up - Tom looks up
in the direction of the NOISE - listening. The motor is HEARD
again. The deer suddenly takes off; immediately Tom follows,
disappearing into the thicket.

MOUNTAIN ROAD - NEAR WHITNEY PORTAL - The Scout drives along the narrow road. Paul occasionally using the binoculars.

MOUNTAIN LAKE - A beautiful spot. Tom comes into view at a half-run; he stops at the bank of the lake and looks back. The Scout can be HEARD in the distance. Tom listens; he enters the lake and begins to swim for the far shore, using the characteristic paddle-strokes of a dog, far different from before in the pool.

THE FAR BANK - Tom wades ashore, shakes himself - and again we are reminded of a large dog emerging from the water. He runs to the forest and disappears among the trees and shrubbery.

MOUNTAIN ROAD - TRAVELING SHOT - The Scout is driving down a narrow mountain road built on the side of a deep, broad gorge. The mountainside across the gorge can be seen.

FROM SCOUT POV as it moves past the trees.

ANGLE - The woods thin out; the opposite mountainside is completely in the clear; directly ahead - and far below stretches Owens Valley. Suddenly Hays points.

> HAYS
> There, sir...there he is.

Wilson stops the Scout; Paul looks through the field glasses.

PANNING SHOT - BINOCULAR POV - PART OF THE SPARSELY VEGETATED MOUNTAINSIDE

> HAYS
> Way down...to the left. Five o'clock.

The binoculars PAN as directed; suddenly it catches a tiny lone figure in its field, scrambling over the rocky ground; it is Tom; he disappears around a rock outcropping.

ANGLE - Paul turns to Wilson.

> PAUL
> Go!

Wilson starts the Scout and takes off down the road.

MOUNTAIN ROAD - VARIOUS SHOTS of the ride down Mt. Whitney, seen from the Scout. The Scout careens down the narrow road; lurches around hairpin curves inches away from thousand-foot drops; below at the bottom of the mountain cliffs lies the expanse of the valley.

FLATLANDS OF ALABAMA HILLS - The Scout comes racing into picture; it stops; in the b.g. we see Mt. Whitney...Paul sweeps the horizon with his field glasses; looks at the men and shakes his head negatively.

                              PAUL
          Lost him, Dammit!

                              HAYS
          We'd better get to the Major soon -- or he's
          gonna kill himself.

                                                  CUT TO:

EXT. SWIMMING POOL - DAY

CLOSE SHOT - WHITE TELEPHONE - A luxuriously landscaped pool area
beyond the telephone standing on a small table; the lush
vegetation spells California. The phone RINGS; a man's bare arm
reaches for the receiver and picks it up. We do not see the man
himself.

                              MAN
          Yes.
                    (listens)
          Yes. Understood.

The hand hangs up the phone, and immediately again removes the
receiver. A finger punches out a number. The phone RINGS a
couple of times.

                              VOICE
          Yes.

                              MAN
          Six, five...Four, two...Seven, nine.

                              VOICE
          Five, eight...

INTERCUT: ARTIST'S STUDIO - DAY

The place is cluttered with finished and partly-finished sketches
and water colors. A MAN is standing at an easel on which is a
nearly finished California scene. He is holding a receiver to
his ear. We see only his shoulder and the back of his head.

                              ARTIST
          ...One, three...Two, six.

RESUME - SWIMMING POOL - DAY

                              MAN AT POOL
          Rendezvous at point Fox. One hour.

                              ARTIST (O.S.)
          Understood.

The man hangs up. Once again he at once removes the receiver and
punches out a number. A different voice from before - answers.

                    VOICE
          Yes.

                    MAN AT POOL
          Six, five...four...

                                        CUT TO:

INT. HOWELL'S OFFICE - DAY

Col. Howell is seated behind his desk; before him sit Randi and
MAJOR ARTHUR TRAFFORD. Randi is greatly troubled. Trafford, an
officer in the Air Medical Corps, is a man in his fifties.

                    HOWELL
          The search-and-rescue effort is already under
          way. Paul is in charge. We have a medical
          officer on the job, too. We'll find Tom -
          even if his actions are - unpredictable.

                    RANDI
          How -- how bad *is* he, John?

Howell evades a direct answer.

                    HOWELL
          I'll personally supervise the entire opera-
          tion, Randi. We'll do the best we can --
          under the circumstances, we --

                    RANDI
          Circumstances? What circumstances?

                    HOWELL
          Tom is not just another pilot down. We have
          to consider his -- his state of mind.

                    RANDI
          What's *wrong* with his mind? John --

Major Trafford suddenly speaks in a calm, authoritative voice.

                    TRAFFORD
          Colonel Howell. I wonder if I might talk to
          Mrs. Darby for a moment?

He looks steadily at Howell. Howell glares at him; he is about
to cut him off; he glances at Randi; he realizes what Trafford is
doing; he nods curtly.

                    TRAFFORD
          Mrs. Darby. Randi, is it?
               (she nods)
                                        MORE

TRAFFORD (Cont'd)
Randi -- I'm a neuro-surgeon. I've already looked over all of the available information about your husband, very closely. Let me try to explain it to you.

Trafford's manner is soothing, calming.

TRAFFORD
From examining Tom's helmet we know <u>where</u> his injury is located. He probably has a fractured skull and a severe cerebral concussion.

Randi reacts sharply.

TRAFFORD
Medical terms, Randi. Sound much worse than they are.

RANDI
But -- why should that make Tom act so -- strangely.

TRAFFORD
We can't know for certain, without an examination -- but it seems that the pressure of the broken bone on Tom's brain and the probable subdural hemorrhage...internal bleeding, have impaired the vulnerable higher brain centers. Where memory, judgment and learned skills are seated.

The tears well in Randi's eyes.

TRAFFORD
Tom is still able to function on a -- eh, biological level. But the integration capacity of the higher brain centers is lost -- in fact producing what we know as total amnesia. Amnestic aphasia. That means the loss of power of speech. -- Absolutely no memory of his past life.

RANDI
Then -- what's left?

TRAFFORD
Only his senses, Randi. And his basic instincts. His native intelligence. But everything he experiences now must be totally new -- and frightening to him. This kind of amnesia can be cured by surgery. If we can get to him on time.

                    RANDI
          ...John, you've got to find him!...What can I
          do?

                    TRAFFORD
          It's quite possible that the sight of you -
          the sound of your voice, perhaps, might break
          through to him.

                    RANDI
          Of course I'll go.

                    HOWELL
          I've just had a report from Paul. Tom is
          headed for the desert - in the direction of
          Death Valley.

                                            DISSOLVE TO:

EXT. DRY LAKE - SUNSET

The expanse of the dry lake lies before us, in the distance a
lonely figure trudges across the desolation. It is Tom...

ANGLE ON TOM - making his way across the dry lake; he glances
back every now and then.

                                            DISSOLVE TO:

EXT. DESERT - NIGHT

Tom comes to a small rise in the desert floor; he is exhausted.

HIGH PANNING SHOT - Tom is resting against the rise; we see that
it is a long, straight embankment; on top of it railroad tracks
stretch away into the distance. CAMERA PANS along the track.
Far away, a single, bright pinpoint of light grows imperceptibly
bigger.

ANGLE ON TOM as he sits up with a start. We HEAR the growing
rumble of an approaching train. Tom jumps up, alert and tense.
He looks around and climbs up on the embankment; he sees the
light...Slowly he begins to back away from it in fear...

ALONG THE TRACKS. The blinding light of the train is rapidly
approaching. Tom is between it and the CAMERA on the tracks. He
begins to run from the onrushing train along the tracks toward
CAMERA, imprisoned in the headlight - like an animal caught in
the headlights of a car, racing ahead of it instead of turning
off the road...

PANNING. Tom is racing in desperate fear along the tracks; the
all-enveloping SOUND of the train comes closer and closer;
suddenly there is an eerie, shrieking BLAST of a horn from the
engine. Tom leaps in an attempt to double his frantic speed.

ON TOM - ALONG TRACKS. The train comes roaring on. At the last possible moment, Tom veers off the tracks and runs past CAMERA in a CLOSE-UP. His eyes are dilated with panic; his mouth split open in a wild scream -- which is utterly drowned out as the train THUNDERS by in a crescendo of noise.

EXT. THE DESERT - NIGHT (MOON). Tom has panicked; he is rushing head-long through the night desert. The roar of the train is dying in the distance. He runs through a stand of grotesque Joshua trees; terror grips him.

TOM'S POV. Tom (THE CAMERA) runs through the grove of Joshua trees; their limbs seem to reach and grope for him.

BACK ON TOM as he comes racing between the trees. Close to CAMERA, he falls to the ground, his face filled with terror; he buries his face in the sand...Then -- with a tremendous effort, he looks up toward the distant safety of the hills.

THE DESERT - TOM'S POV. The mountains loom in the b.g. But a short distance away, two large, dark objects can be seen, huddled among the vegetation.

ON TOM as he starts to crawl toward the objects...

TRUCK AND HORSE-TRAILER pulled off the road...All is quiet.

INT. TRUCK CAB

A Mexican, JOSE, and his young son, RAMON, are sleeping in the cab.

EXT. HORSE-TRAILER

The back of it is covered with a canvas flap. Tom comes up to it; he crawls into this iron cave.

INT. HORSE TRAILER

It is empty. Tom crawls in through the flap. There is straw on the floor - and a bulging sack sits in one corner. Tom seeks a resting place; he draws his knees up to his chin and almost at once falls into a coma-like sleep.

SMASH TO:

INT. LABORATORY PROJECTION ROOM - SCREEN - NIGHT

A piece of military hardware literally disintegrates in a loud, crackling explosion and a blinding fireball. Gen. Ryan, Marcus and Harnum are sitting in the small, security-guarded screening room, grimly watching the projected scenes of awesome power. There will be a couple of spectacular shots of laser beams burning through inch-thick steel and destroying military hardware.

HARNUM
          These are the early experiments, General.
          We'll come to the tests of the Marcus beam in
          a moment. It will be employed with the EMG
          sight as in the flight.

Ryan acknowledges as he watches. All the men tense as the Marcus device tests begin. The proper Air Force designations appear on the screen - and the word SECRET. A clock is racing in the corner of the frame, showing the delay between firing the missiles and the impacts...Then the legend XM-9, MARCUS flashes on the screen - and we see a series of _static_ tests of the device:

Tom is seated in a static test set in the ground test bunker; he is wearing the EMG sight helmet...Before him on the firing range are several targets in the distance, watched by the observers through binoculars; tanks, planes, bunkers, etc. Tom has a weapon firing grip in his hand - and the XM-9 high particle power beam is encased in a static housing nearby.

We see how Tom "sights" in on the targets (two moving cross-hairs on his little sighting screen that intersect on the target at which he looks). When he presses the firing button there is a flash too quick to identify as a beam - and the target he looked at instantly disintegrates. The clock in the corner of the frame does not have time to register at all!

When the scene goes black after the display of pure power, Ryan turns to Marcus.

                    RYAN
          Any ideas?

Marcus shakes his head.

                    MARCUS
          I still see nothing that can shed any
          light...
                    (he frowns)
          Of course - the static test with a ground-
          secured power plant _is_ different from an
          airborne mission.

                    RYAN
          Then - Major Darby is the key.

                    HARNUM
          The only one, I'm afraid.

                                                            CUT TO:

EXT. IRAQ COUNTRYSIDE - LONG SHOT - DAY

A military vehicle is driving toward a large industrial plant.

EXT. PLANT ENTRY GATE

Signs in Arabic and English identify the plant as an Asphalt Processing Plant. The buildings are all sooty black and surrounded by industrial machinery. The military vehicle is admitted and drives up to the main building. Two Iraqi officers dismount and enter.

INT. PLANT - CORRIDOR

The two officers walk down the corridor which is immaculately clean. It is obvious that this is not an asphalt processing facility - the international atomic radiation sign is everywhere. The two officers stop at door marked in Arabic: DR. WILHELM KREBBS, PROJECT ENGINEER. They enter without knocking.

INT. KREBB'S OFFICE

A man in a white coat is working at a drafting table. He is in his late sixties, obviously Caucasian.

> OFFICER
> You are Doctor Wilhelm Krebbs?

> KREBBS
> (apprehensively)
> I am. What --

> OFFICER
> You are to come with us.

CUT TO:

INT. COL. GERHARDT SCHARFF'S OFFICE - DAY

Col. Scharff is sitting at his desk, working. There is a KNOCK on the door. Without looking up from his work, Scharff answers curtly:

> SCHARFF
> Come!

There is the SOUND of a door opening and people entering. The door closes. Scharff keeps writing - then he looks up.

KREBBS - TWO OFFICERS - SCHARFF'S POV - Krebbs looks apprehensive.

ANGLE ON SCHARFF - He breaks into a smile - not a pleasant sight.

> SCHARFF
> Ah! Doctor Krebbs.

He gets up. CAMERA CARRIES him around the desk to Krebbs. The two officers leave.

SCHARFF
Sit down, Herr Doktor, sit down.
(pours from a carafe)
I am sure you will not mind a little brandy.

Krebbs accepts a glass; he is non-plussed. Scharff hefts his glass.

SCHARFF
Zum wohl, Herr Doktor!

KREBBS
Thank you, Herr...?

SCHARFF
Forgive me, Herr Doktor Krebbs. I am Colonel Gerhardt Scharff, Foreign Intelligence. Special Advisor to His Excellency the President. Formerly of the Gestapo.

Krebbs looks startled. Scharff leans toward him.

SCHARFF
I shall be brief, Herr Doktor. You were an associate of Doctor Werner von Braun, were you not?

KREBBS
(startled)
I was. I...

SCHARFF
How long have you been working on His Excellency's - nuclear weapon project?

KREBBS
Eight years.

SCHARFF
(he nods)
I know His Excellency is pleased.

He lets the sentence hang.

KREBBS
Thank you, Herr Oberst.

SCHARFF
When you were developing the V-2 rocket with von Braun, you had a colleague named Marcus, yes?

KREBBS
Yes. Doctor Theodor Marcus. I-I have not been in contact with him since - since...

SCHARFF
Peenemünde. Quite. Working with the
Americans, Doctor Marcus has developed a
certain device for them. A device to be
mounted on their latest fighter aircraft. A
device that could be of immeasurable
importance to His Excellency.

KREBBS
I - see...
    (he doesn't)

SCHARFF
There is a possibility that we <u>may</u> come into
possession of this, eh, <u>Marcus device</u>. In
what state is unfortunately impossible to
tell...

KREBBS
But - I...

SCHARFF
Now, Herr Doktor. Straight to the point. If
we should find ourselves in a position to
furnish you with - eh, certain material -
what would you need to be able to - to
reconstruct the work of Dr. Marcus?

KREBBS
Notes...Theo's - Doctor Marcus' notes. They-

Scharff makes a negative gesture.

KREBBS
Or, perhaps an operations manual - a repair
manual. That sort of thing. Procurement
orders...Someone who had worked on the
project. Or - the pilot of the plane that
carries it. He would have had to be
thoroughly familiar with it in order to test
it effectively.

Scharff sits up, suddenly wholly interested.

SCHARFF
The pilot??

KREBBS
That would certainly have been the case at
Peenemünde...If we could question the pilot,
we might learn enough to accomplish a great
deal...Herr Oberst. This - device. I shall
have to know what its purpose is.

Scharff looks quickly at him; he frowns; then he looks up at Krebbs - and smiles.

                    SCHARFF
        Yes. You will - won't you? Doctor Marcus
        has developed a Laser Activated Energy Beam.
        A particle beam. Extremely powerful. The
        Americans call it the XM-9. Coupled with
        their new eye-movement sight, this device has
        the capability to destroy any attacking
        missile, rocket or aircraft.

He lets his words sink in. Krebbs is watching him intently.

                    SCHARFF
        Instantaneous, infallible, intercept, Herr
        Doctor. And total destruction. We know the
        result of complete air superiority. The
        American 'Desert Storm'...
            (he makes his words sound like swear words)
        ...taught us that. But - if _we_ had this
        latest generation Marcus device, it would be
        a different story next time.

                                                          CUT TO:

EXT. DESERT - ON TRUCK AND HORSE-TRAILER - SUNRISE

INT. TRUCK CAB

The sun is hitting Jose's face. He wakes up and yawns. His son, Ramon, eight, wakes up, too. Jose starts up the truck.

INT. HORSE-TRAILER

Tom wakes up with a start, the RUMBLE of the engine loud in his ears. He springs to a crouch. Suddenly the trailer lurches as it is driven up onto the road. Tom reacts in terror - as the trailer gathers speed. He creeps to the tail end flap and peers out.

TOM'S POV. The ground is racing away from the trailer.

ANGLE ON TOM. Terrified, he retreats to a far corner and huddles there.

EXT. DESERT ROAD - DAY

The truck towing the horse-trailer is speeding down the road.

INT. TRUCK CAB

Jose and Ramon are driving along.

EXT. ROAD THROUGH HILLS

The truck comes driving along. CAMERA PANS with it, coming to rest on a road sign that reads: DEATH VALLEY NATIONAL MONUMENT.

INT. TRAILER

Tom is huddled in a corner. Some of his terror has left him.

EXT. ROAD TO DEATH VALLEY (190)

The truck and trailer are careening along the road. Ahead lies the vast, desolate expanse of Death Valley...

INT. TRAILER

Tom stirs; he is attracted (by smell) to the bulky sack in the other corner. He rips the sacking; several oranges spill out. He picks one up; he smells it; he bites into it. He reacts to the bitter rind - but discovers the sweet insides; he greedily eats the moist pulp.

EXT. DESERT ROAD IN DEATH VALLEY

It is deserted. The truck and trailer are barrelling down the road.

INT. TRUCK CAB

      RAMON
 Papa. I got to pee.

      JOSE
 Okay. Me, too.

He slows and stops. Ramon scampers out. Jose starts to open his door. He catches sight of the rearview mirror mounted there.

      JOSE
 What the hell...?

ANGLE ON MIRROR. In it, Tom is seen running from the rear of the trailer, racing into the desert toward the foothills.

              CUT TO:

EXT. DEATH VALLEY NATIONAL MONUMENT RANGER HEADQUARTERS - DAY

Several military and ranger vehicles are parked outside.

CLOSE SHOT - SIGN OVER ENTRANCE. It reads:

    DEATH VALLEY NATIONAL MONUMENT
      RANGER HEADQUARTERS
        Elevation
     150 Feet Below Sea Level

INT. CHIEF RANGER STARK'S OFFICE

It is a large room; on one wall is a large map of the entire Death Valley area; on the other walls a few framed photographs of Death Valley scenes...Paul and Ward are at a desk, talking earnestly; CHIEF RANGER STARK is at another desk going over some papers with a RANGER. Colonel Howell and Major Trafford stride into the room. The men start to get up.

HOWELL
Sit down!

His manner is even more brusque than usual. He walks to the wall map; studies it for a moment - then turns sharply to the men.

HOWELL
Two days - and no results!

PAUL
This is no ordinary rescue operation, or we'd have picked up Tom long ago.

WARD
We're doing the best we can.

HOWELL
Not good enough! Have you any idea where he is?

PAUL
No, sir, we don't...we--

HOWELL
Well, I do!
(slams his fist on the map)
Here! Right smack in the middle of Death Valley!

PAUL
Here? How could he have possibly have traveled that far?

HOWELL
Chief Ranger Stark just had a report. From an irate citizen of Mexican descent. Claims a hitchhiker - a weird hombre, as he put it - stole him blind. Ate a whole sack of his oranges.

TOM
Tom? A hitchhiker?

HOWELL
Stowaway is more the word. He holed up in an empty horse-trailer on its way here.

PAUL
Two million acres of desolation...Colonel Howell...We need a lot more men to cover this area.

WARD
Time is of the essence.

HOWELL
You've got your search teams and choppers. And Stark has pledged his full cooperation. That will have to do.

PAUL
(rebelling)
Why?

HOWELL
I don't want Tom to kill himself.

TRAFFORD
Maybe I can clarify that a little. You know, Paul, that some wild animals when cornered, will try to destroy themselves rather than be captured. Or attempt to do impossible things that result in their destruction...

HOWELL
That is the reason for no large-scale man-hunt. We cannot afford to make him desperate.

PAUL
What about Randi? Why was she brought up here?

HOWELL
Major Trafford and I feel she can be of help. Communicate with her husband when he's located.

PAUL
Okay. As long as she stays out of the way.

HOWELL
You don't understand. Mrs. Darby is to be available to communicate with her husband - in the field. She will accompany you.

PAUL
What the hell am I going to do with a female tagging along?

                    HOWELL
          I expect you to follow the best cause of
          action to reach Major Darby! And that
          includes taking his wife along on the search.

                    TRAFFORD
               (conciliatory)
          Where is Randi now?

                    HOWELL
          Over at the ranch.

                    TRAFFORD
          It will be tough on her, but she can be of
          use. When Tom is sighted.

                    HOWELL
          You had better plan your next moves. In this
          damn heat Tom won't last long without water.
          And water is hard to come by in this god-
          forsaken place...
               (looks at Paul)
          I suggest you start looking. Now!

                                                  CUT TO:

EXT. DEATH VALLEY - DAY

MONTAGE of USAF Scouts and ranger vehicles as they search the
valley, driving through spectacular locations...and search
through ghost towns and abandoned mine areas...The feeling is of
a huge, forbidding place - a herculean task.

EXT. STEEP ROAD

A Scout is laboring up the incline; Paul is driving; Randi sits
next to him and Hays is in the back...A ranger pickup with ADAMS
at the wheel is following...

ANOTHER ANGLE. The Scout pulls over and stops - the ranger truck
behind it. Paul turns to Hays.

                    PAUL
          Sergeant. Get lost for a moment.

                    HAYS
          Yes, sir.

He climbs out and goes over to the ranger truck.

                    PAUL
          Listen, Randi. I might as well be blunt. I
          want you to know you're here over my objec-
          tions.
               (she listens in grim silence)   MORE

                    PAUL (Cont'd)
          As you can see, it's not going to be a picnic
          up here.

                    RANDI
          I'm not here to have a picnic.

                    PAUL
          This is <u>my</u> job, Randi. And I know my job.
          There's nothing you can do that I can't do.

                    RANDI
          Let me be blunt, too, Paul. I think there
          is. And I'm here to do whatever I can. I'll
          keep up with you - or you can send me back.

For a moment he looks at her, then he snaps.

                    PAUL
          You got it!
                    (he calls)
          Sergeant! Let's go!

Hays runs to the Scout and jumps in; the two vehicles drive off.

                                              CUT TO:

EXT. ZABRISKIE POINT

The vehicles arrive at the parking area. The men dismount and
look around. Spread out before them lie the spectacular Black
Mountains, cut through with deep ravines and washes.

                    PAUL
          Adams. Take the right. I'll take the left.

The two men begin to search the eroded hills with their field
glasses.

BINOCULAR SHOTS as Paul and Adams sweep the desolate slopes with
their field glasses. There is no one to be seen.

ANGLE ON PAUL as he is looking down into a wash far below.
Suddenly he starts.

BINOCULAR SHOT - PAUL'S POV. Rounding a bend on the distant
wash, a tiny figure comes plodding along. It is Tom!

                    PAUL (O.S.)
          There he is!

ON PAUL

                    PAUL
          My God! There he is!

The men converge on Paul, and Randi tumbles from the Scout.

                      PAUL
               (gruffly)
      Okay, Randi, you're on. Go ahead. Call to
      him. Shout! As loud as you can.

Randi runs to the parapet surrounding the area.

                      RANDI
      Tom!...Tom!...It's me!

Far below Tom draws up - and looks up at the people above.

                      RANDI (O.S.)
      Darling...It's me!...<u>Randi</u>!

ON TOM as he is looking up at the sound; angry defiance is building on his sun-scorched face - mixed with fear and confusion - but there is no recognition...For a brief moment he listens - then he abruptly turns around and runs back the way he came.

                      RANDI (O.S.)
             (faintly)
      Tom!...Wait!

RANDI AND OTHERS

                      RANDI
      Please!...

She gives up; she looks defeated; she whispers.

                      RANDI
      Please...Please. Tom - wait...
             (turns to Paul)
      He didn't know me at all...

Paul looks at her; his compassion shows through his gruffness.

                      PAUL
      Perhaps he couldn't hear you...Or didn't
      recognize your voice. It's a long way down
      there.

He is not convinced himself, but Randi clings to the shred of hope.

                      RANDI
      Then we'll just have to get closer to him.

Paul strides to the ranger pickup; Adams already has a map spread out on the hood.

                    PAUL
          Adams. How do we get down there? Fast? Cut
          him off?

                    ADAMS
          We can't get through to him from here.
          Perhaps one of the other units...on foot...

Paul turns toward Hays standing at the Scout radio.

                    PAUL
          Hays! Get Major Ward!

He hurries over; Hays is on the radio.

                    HAYS
          Armadillo Two. This is Armadillo One. Come
          in...come in...

The radio SPUTTERS; Hays repeats his call - then:

                    RADIO
          This is Armadillo Two. Go ahead.

Paul grabs the mike.

                    PAUL
          Ward. We've spotted him. He's headed for
          Desolation Canyon...Close in. We'll join
          you...

EXT. DESERT ROAD - DAY

ANGLE ON WARD'S SCOUT parked near the foothills. Ward is on the radio; Wilson behind the wheel.

                    WARD
          Roger, Armadillo One. Leaving immediately.
          Out.

The Scout takes off in a cloud of dust.

ANGLE ON VEHICLES AT ZABRISKIE POINT as they roar off...

EXT. WASH

ANGLE ON TOM as he is half-running along. He stops. Ahead of him the hills grow steeper. He hesitates - then <u>reverses direction</u>, runs a short distance and disappears into the gully of a contributory wash...

                                                  CUT TO:

EXT. RANGER HEADQUARTERS

Two Scouts come driving up. Paul, Ward and Randi dismount. From the building Stark and three men emerge. Stark walks up to Paul.

                    STARK
          I don't have to ask.

                    PAUL
          We had to go on foot. We lost him.

He nods toward Hays and Wilson, driving the Scouts off.

                    PAUL
          We'll gas up - and take off again.

                    STARK
          I'm bringing my complement up to emergency
          strength. Got a few new men.
                    (he nods toward the three men with him)

                    PAUL
          Right. Thanks.

                    STARK
          I'll have them in the field in no time.
                    (he looks at Paul)
          You know, Tom may be moving at night. When
          it's cooler.

                    PAUL
          Howell's putting one of the new rescue
          choppers on the project. They'll start
          tonight.

Stark nods. He gestures to his men; they walk off as Paul turns to talk to Randi.

ANGLE ON NEW RANGERS as they follow Stark.

ANGLE ON RANGER GORDON as he pauses and looks toward Paul.

                    STARK (O.S.)
          Come on, Gordon!

The ranger walks on.

RANDI AND PAUL as Ward joins them; the two men walk into the building; Randi starts to walk toward a little grove of twisted withered trees close by; she looks tired and dejected.

ANGLE ON TRAFFORD outside the HQ building, leaning against the wall, smoking a pipe; he looks after Randi, taps out his pipe, puts it in his pocket - and starts toward the little grove.

ON RANDI sitting on a tree. She looks up as Trafford approaches.
CAMERA WIDENS.

                    TRAFFORD
          Randi. You look beat. Why don't you lie
          down a while? Out of the heat.

                    RANDI
          I'll just sit here for a minute. I'm fine.

But her appearance belies her words. Trafford sits down near
her.

                    TRAFFORD
          Are you...?

Randi puts her hands to her face; she is obviously under great
strain.

                    TRAFFORD
          You mustn't give up, Randi. They'll find
          him.

Randi looks up.

                    RANDI
          It isn't that - it's...

She stops suddenly. Trafford looks up sharply; he speaks gently.

                    TRAFFORD
          <u>What</u> is it, Randi?

Randi's barriers suddenly collapse.

                    RANDI
          It's <u>my</u> fault Tom crashed. It's all my
          fault...if he dies.

                    TRAFFORD
          That's quite a responsibility you're taking
          on. Why do you feel that way?

                    RANDI
          Because he was worried. Because he didn't -
          <u>couldn't</u> concentrate. He may have done
          something wrong - and crashed...because of
          me.

                    TRAFFORD
          Why Randi?

On the verge of losing control, with a conscious effort, she
pulls herself together.

                    RANDI
          Because for months our marriage hasn't been a
          marriage...

Trafford watches her with growing comprehension - but deliberately stays silent.

                    RANDI
          ...I don't know what happened to me...I - Yes
          - I do know! I lost the baby! After carry-
          ing it for more than eight months - I lost
          it...

Randi shudders; she stares at Trafford - past him - not seeing
him - through him into a nightmare, remembered by a pain-inflamed
mind. CAMERA DOLLIES IN to a CLOSE-UP of Randi, during:

                    RANDI
                 (tonelessly)
          I was lying there. Alone. For hours.
          Waiting. But he was away...I knew I would
          lose the baby...I knew...I knew--

FLASHBACK TO: THE DARBY HOME - THE NURSERY - DAY

The nursery contains all the things for the awaited baby
including a crib, a gaily painted dresser and stuffed toys.
Randi, obviously pregnant, stands on a small ladder/stool
reaching to hang a mobile on a hook in the ceiling over the
crib...She suddenly loses her balance; she starts to fall - the
mobile flying from her hands...

POV RANDI. SLOW MOTION. The room, the crib, the dresser, the
animal toys, the ceiling all whirl around crazily as she falls.

ON RANDI. SLOW MOTION. She is falling from the stool; she hits
her stomach on the corner of the crib...

ON RANDI. She struggles to her feet, steadying herself on the
dresser. She places her hands on her swollen belly; her face is
contorted with agony; she looks down...

FLOOR. POV RANDI. On the carpet between her feet a few bright
red spots of blood appear.

ON RANDI. She collapses. Lying on the floor she strains to look
toward the door. She screams - a silent sound.

DOOR. POV RANDI. It seems to swim - forbidding, silent, closed
- in space...And the SCENE GOES BLACK...Struggling up from the
stygian abyss the scene slowly reappears. It is now NIGHT. The
DOOR, closed, is suddenly opened, and silhouetted against the
light in the hall stands TOM. He hurries to Randi - to a
distorted CLOSE-UP; he looks shocked...

ON RANDI. She reaches out for Tom; she screams soundlessly and
throws back her head in agony; she strains in desperation...

SHOT - RANDI'S POV - THE CRIB. CAMERA starts on an EXTREME
CLOSE-UP of one of the staves in the crib side; it PANS along the
crib side - increasing speed - until it is racing along the
staves to a SHOT of the top of the dresser seemingly an eternity
above...

The scene swims to BLACK...It comes back to a dark, formless shape moving...The shape becomes Tom, RANDI'S POV; he is holding his Air Force uniform jacket bundled up in front of him; he looks grief-stricken; he bends over Randi (CAMERA)...and again the scene goes BLACK.

BACK TO TRAFFORD AND RANDI. She has her hands in front of her face; she slowly removes them...

                    RANDI
    She was dead...The baby was dead...

She takes a deep breath; she looks bleakly at Trafford.

                    RANDI
    And after that, everything fell apart. I
    couldn't stand Tom touching me. I'd see him
    standing there...I - I just freeze up every
    time he comes near me...Sometimes I even
    think I blame him for the baby's death...

She stops, horrified at her own words. Trafford remains silent.

                    RANDI
        (with a sob)
    I don't mean that! It doesn't make sense. I
    <u>do</u> love him...But now - I don't even think I
    can be of any help...I saw him...I called to
    him...He didn't react at all...And the night
    before he --

She stops.

                    TRAFFORD
    He what - Randi?

                    RANDI
    He wanted me. And I...I - Look what I've
    done to him.

                    TRAFFORD
    Tom had an accident. What went wrong up
    there was beyond your control. What's
    happened between you is in no way to blame
    for that - or for Tom's condition.

                    RANDI
    I want very much to believe that. If only we
    could find him.

                    TRAFFORD
    We will.

                              RANDI
                    I guess - Tom and I - we're both a little
                    lost.

                                                  SMASH TO:

EXT. FOOTHILLS - EFFECT SHOT - DAY

A moped comes ROARING past CAMERA, closely followed by a second
moped. The mufflers have been fixed to make maximum noise.

ANGLE - MOPED DRIVERS. Two BOYS (16-17) are racing down the
desert dirt road, clowning and stunting on their mopeds. One of
the boys happens to look toward the foothills not too far away
from the road, he reacts:

                              BOY ONE
                    Hey! What's that?
                         (points)
                    Over there...by the gorge...See it?

                              BOY TWO
                    Yeah...What the hell is it?

                              BOY ONE
                    Looks like a spaced out O.M.

                              BOY TWO
                    That's no old man.

                              BOY ONE
                    Well, he sure's no superjock. He looks
                    wrecked.

They strain to see.

EXTREME LONG SHOT - BOYS' POV. In the far distance, a crouched
"figure" can be seen moving slowly out of a narrow gorge. It is
Tom.

ANGLE ON BOYS

                              BOY ONE
                    Come on. Drop the hammer!

The two boys start up their mopeds and race down a trail toward
the foothills.

ON TOM. Exhausted, sweat-dirty, clothes in tatters, he looks up
in sudden, wild alarm, as the NOISE of the mopeds approaching
across the desert reaches him. He starts to back away...

ANGLE ON MOPEDS as they race toward Tom.

ON TOM looking trapped; he begins to run along the foothills...

MOPEDS as they turn to head Tom off.

ANGLE ON TOM running along the foothills nearing a break; the two mopeds are racing after him. He slips on the rocks; he gets up - and crouched on his haunches, his hands on the ground - he turns his wild face toward the oncoming mopeds as he gathers his strength. The boys on the mopeds draw up and stop.

ON BOYS. They stare at the strange "creature" some distance before them.

                    BOY ONE
     Man! What kind of weirdo is that?

                    BOY TWO
     Looks like a fugitive from a funny farm.

                    BOY ONE
     Let's go put a net over him!

He guns his moped; they ROAR off.

ANGLE ON TOM. The ROAR of the mopeds LOUD in his ears, he leaps to his feet and streaks for the break in the foothills.

CORNERING AND ATTACK SEQUENCE

The boys on their mopeds ROAR after the fleeing Tom. He enters a ravine with a perpendicular wall on one side and steep slope on the other; it is strewn with boulders...The racing mopeds easily overtake Tom; one drives past and turns; they have him boxed... Tom desperately seeks a way out...The boys, at first startled at his wild appearance, are having fun "herding" Tom between them, gunning their noisy mopeds...Finally they have him trapped between them, his back against the perpendicular wall...Tom - his lips drawn back in a snarl - faces them...Suddenly - with the desperation of a cornered rat - he leaps for one of the mopeds, a scream of fury tearing from his throat...Taken by surprise, the boy on the moped tries to avoid his charge; he guns his moped and loses control - and the vehicle crashes into a boulder - hurling the boy head-first into the rock...He slips limply to the ground...Tom runs to the machine. With unbridled fury he attacks - not the boy, but the moped, the monster that has been tormenting him...With superhuman strength, he lifts it up - and slams it violently into the rock...The gas tank splits, and at once flames shoot up around the wrecked frame...

Tom whirls on the other rider...Petrified, the boy guns his moped...Turning it away he finds himself headed for the steep slope; he tries to scale it...Gravel and rocks spew from his spinning wheels. Suddenly the vehicle bucks; it pitches over backward - and tumbles down the slope, the boy after...

The moped hurtles down the slope; it crashes into the burning bike at the boulder - and an EXPLOSION rocks the ravine...

Tom is thrown to the ground...At once he gets up - and flees - leaving behind two still figures sprawled on the ground and a blazing fire sending billows of black smoke into the air...

EXT. DESERT ROAD - DAY

Ward's Scout with Wilson driving is coming down the road. It stops. Wilson points ahead.

        WILSON
 Look!

SHOT - WARD'S AND WILSON'S POV. In the distance a column of black smoke rises over the foothills.

ANGLE ON SCOUT as it takes off in the direction of the smoke.

                 CUT TO:

INT. RANGER HEADQUARTERS - DAY

CLOSE ON a wall map; a hand comes into the picture and points to a spot; CAMERA PULLS BACK to reveal Ward. Paul and Stark standing in front of the wall map.

        WARD
 Here...Here's where he attacked the two moped
 drivers from the trailer camp.

        PAUL
  (grim-faced)
 Attacked?

        WARD
 I know. It sounds - unbelievable...But...
 Fact is, we've got one kid with a fractured
 skull and another with a broken collar bone
 and a hide covered with contusions and
 lacerations.

Scowling, Paul turns to the map.

        PAUL
 Here's where we lost him...And here's where
 you found the mopeds.
  (turns back to the others)
 We'll place observers in a ring around that
 area.
  (again points to the map)
 Here...here...here...and here.
  (turns to Stark)
 Tell your men to keep their eyes open.

        STARK
 They'll spot him. If he's still there.

PAUL
We'll patrol the area - ready to move in as
soon as they do. Get on it...

Stark leaves. Ward turns soberly to Paul.

WARD
He's getting dangerous, Paul.

PAUL
Meaning?

WARD
Meaning that we'd better get him - before he
really attacks someone...Or kills them.

Paul looks at him, his face grim. Randi enters. Paul turns to her.

RANDI
Are you going out?

PAUL
Yes.

RANDI
I'm going along.
(Paul starts to protest)
Remember our bargain.

CUT TO:

EXT. MOUNTAIN LOOKOUT POINT - DAY

A ranger truck drives up; a RANGER gets out; he carries a pair of binoculars and a Walkie-Talkie; he takes up his observation post as the trucks drives off.

EXT. STOVEPIPE WELLS GAS STATION - DAY

A Scout driven by Hays comes barrelling down the road and speeds past the gas station.

ANGLE ON STATION. At a coke machine stands a MAN; he looks after the disappearing Scout. A telephone booth can be seen nearby.

CLOSE SHOT. With a <u>booted foot</u>, the man kicks an empty coke can...

EXT. VALLEY FLOOR - DAY

A ranger jeep is parked off the road. Ranger Gordon stands by it, watching the foothills through his binoculars. He gets into the jeep and takes off.

CUT TO:

EXT. HIGH SCENIC SPOT - DAY

Two scouts and two rangers are parked together; around them - sweating in the scorching sun - are Paul, Randi, Ward, Hays, Wilson, Adams and two rangers.

ON PAUL AND RANDI sitting together looking out over the valley. Paul, hot and sweaty, watches Randi with grudging respect; she's obviously suffering from the heat.

He hands her his canteen; she drinks. For a moment she sits in thought.

                    PAUL

  What is it?

                    RANDI

  Oh, nothing...I - I was just thinking. It's
  so terribly hot and I was so thirsty. I have
  water. What about Tom? What must it be like
  for him?

She squints up at the burning sun overhead.

                                                  CUT TO:

EXT. CANYON ENTRANCE - DAY

ANGLE ON TOM peering in agony up at the relentless sun; his face is sweaty and burned. He licks his cracked lips with a dry tongue and starts off toward the shade offered by some rock outcroppings.

ANOTHER ANGLE ON slope of the alluvial fan stretching out from the narrow gorge. Tom makes his way toward the rugged rock deposits in a staggering half-run. At a dirt road stands a round tank, supported on sturdy wooden beams. Tom makes his way toward it. As he passes it, CAMERA REVEALS the word W A T E R in large letters on the side of the tank. Tom glances at the tank - and struggles on as CAMERA ZOOMS IN on a tap and sign advising people that water is available for radiators and asking them to close the tap firmly after use.

ON TOM staggering along; he falls to his knees; then collapses completely. Lying prostrate on the flash-flood debris. He is exhausted, parched with thirst; he wipes his face with a grimy hand and peers ahead with sun-blinded eyes.

TOM'S POV - CACTUS AND ROCKS. In the distance on the rocky ground stands a large cactus. The picture slips IN and OUT OF FOCUS through the glimmering heat waves rising from the burning desert floor. The rocks cast pools of shade.

ON TOM as he struggles to his feet; he begins to toil toward the cacti – and shade. As he drags himself along, he stumbles and falls with his knee raking across the sharp needles of a small barrel cactus. With sudden rage, he whirls on the pain-inflicting object. With a booted foot, he stamps on it – crushing it.

CLOSE SHOT – CACTUS. In the pulp, beads of moisture are sparkling. Tom falls to his knees; with his hands he scoops up the moist cactus pulp and buries his face in it...

ANOTHER LOCATION. At a crossroad, Gordon's jeep turns toward the mountains, entering a narrow road into the foothills.

EXT. ROAD THROUGH FOOTHILLS – DAY

The sides are steep but not unscalable; the road winds through the hills. Gordon's jeep is driving slowly; it comes to a stop.

ANGLE ON GORDON as he disembarks. We see that he wears heavy boots. He walks a few steps along the road; stops – and listens. All is quiet. He is just about to turn – when there is the RUSTLE of stones; he freezes. Ahead of him a few small rocks trickle down from behind an outcropping. Faint scraping NOISES can be heard. CAMERA WIDENS as the ranger quickly runs back to his jeep; he leans over the front seat.

CLOSE ANGLE – ROCK OUTCROPPING. Gordon is approaching; suddenly a FIGURE tumbles from behind the rock directly at Gordon; startled, the ranger jumps aside – automatically bringing up his gun...The figure – a youngish man with a swarthy complexion and long, black hair and wearing heavy boots – gets up and stares at Gordon.

                    MAN
    Hey, man, don't shoot. I only lost my
    footing.

                    GORDON
    What're you doing up there?

                    MAN
    Working, man. Working.

He looks around, picks up a drawing tablet, lost in his fall.

                    MAN
    I'm making a series of desert sketches. For
    a book...Fantastic!
            (shows the table to Gordon)
    See?

CLOSE-UP – SKETCH

It is a very good one; it shows the view out over the valley.

TWO SHOT

                    GORDON
          You gotta be careful...Especially if you
          travel about the valley alone. An accident
          up here can be serious. Fatal.
                    (looks around)
          How'd you get here?

                    MAN
          In Sarah.

                    GORDON
          Sarah?

                    MAN
          My buggy.
                    (points)
          She's parked around the bend.

                    GORDON
          Just don't block the road.

                    MAN
          Really.

Gordon stalks away. The Artist scowls after him.

                                                  CUT TO:

EXT. CACTUS - DAY

ANGLE ON TOM curled up in the shade of the rocks. His eyes are closed. Suddenly he opens them. He sits up - and looks off; something has alarmed him.

CLOSE-UP - SCORPION

It's lethal tail carried high; it makes a few scurrying motions among the stones.

CLOSE - TOM watching the scorpion with fascination. "Is it something to eat?" He reaches a hand toward the creature.

SCORPION. It scurries away a few inches; it stops, turns and presents its deadly stinger.

TOM. Again he reaches for the scorpion. Suddenly the distant SOUND of laboring engines is heard. Tom is instantly alert - the scorpion forgotten. He gets up into an easy crouch and stares in the direction of the motor sounds.

EXTREME LONG SHOT - TOM'S POV. Below on the valley floor - two vehicles can be seen raising dust clouds as they roar along.

ANGLE ON TOM. He looks around in alarm; the alluvial fan affords no cover for an escape; he glances toward the canyon entrance and begins to run toward it...disappearing into its safety...

ON ROAD. One of the vehicles, a Scout, turns off and heads for the canyon; the other continues.

DISSOLVE TO:

CACTUS STAND. The Scout drives up; Ward and Wilson get out; they examine the crushed cacti; the pulp is still soft.

                    WARD
He's been here. And not too long ago.

                    WILSON
But cactuses can't keep you alive. They only help you die a little slower.

                    WARD
Cacti.

                    WILSON
Whatever. You sure it was the Major?

Ward nods. He looks up the rugged mountains of the canyon.

                    WARD
He may still be here...

They get into the Scout and start into the canyon.

ANGLE ON CANYON. The Scout drives up and stops. Ward and Wilson dismount; they scan the rises above...Suddenly Wilson points.

                    WILSON
Up there, sir! On the ridge...See it?

RIDGE - MEN'S POV. High above the tiny figure of Tom can be seen climbing up.

                    WILSON
Its' the Major, all right!
                      (he calls)
Major!...Major Darby!

ANGLE ON RIDGE. High above Tom looks down - he scrambles for the crest - dislodging several rocks that come trickling down the steep slope.

ANGLE ON MEN BELOW. They shield themselves from the rain of pebbles.

                                WARD
                    It'll be dark in an hour...Wilson. Get on
                    the radio. Notify Captain Jarman we've
                    spotted him.

Both men run to the Scout, Wilson picks up the mike.

                                WILSON
                    Armadillo One...Armadillo One...come in...
                    This is Armadillo...

A growing RUMBLE from above makes them both look up. Down the
slope a huge boulder comes bouncing, gathering an avalanche of
rocks, rushing with increasing speed directly down on them...

The two men leap for cover - as the first boulder crashes into
the Scout...The men run to the Scout; it is totally destroyed -
the radio smashed! Grimly the men trade looks.

                                WARD
                    He's learning...

                                                      CUT TO:

EXT. BAGHDAD - OFFICIAL BUILDING - NIGHT (SAME AS PREVIOUS SHOT)

INT. SCHARFF'S OFFICE

Scharff is sitting at his desk. Suddenly - without a knock - the
door opens and a MAN enters. Scharff looks up in annoyance - but
his expression changes immediately. He springs to his feet.

                                SCHARFF
                    <u>Cedi</u> Minister! I - I didn't --

                                MINISTER
                    Sit down, <u>Molazem</u>.

The man is small of stature and wears pince-nez spectacles. He
has a habit of adjusting them at crucial moments; he has a
deceptively mild-mannered way of speaking, often at variance with
his words. He wears Arab clothing.

                                MINISTER
                    I want facts, <u>Molazem</u>. Not conjecture.

                                SCHARFF
                    Of course, <u>Cedi</u> Minister.

The Minister waves an impatient hand.

                                MINISTER
                    First. That device of Doctor Marcus'. It is
                    destroyed?

                    SCHARFF
          Yes. It is of no possible use to anyone.

                    MINISTER
          Do they know what went wrong?

                    SCARFF
          My information is that they do not know the
          cause of the malfunction.

                    MINISTER
          Your information is reliable?

                    SCHARFF
          We have two agents, both in place. Top men.
          Unknown to each other, of course.

                    MINISTER
          What is your communications set-up?

                    SCHARFF
          Reports every four hours. The agents in the
          field have a contact schedule to be main-
          tained with the L.A. control - using only
          public telephones that cannot be tapped.

                    MINISTER
          Adequate.

                    SCHARFF
          Information and instructions can be exchanged
          within half an hour, Cedi.

                    MINISTER
          The pilot?

Scharff is growing increasingly ill-at-ease.

                    SCHARFF
          Developments are - confusing. It would now
          seem that it is most doubtful if the pilot
          will fall into our hands.

The Minister adjusts his pince-nez eyeglasses; a gesture not lost
on Scharff.

                    MINISTER
          So, Molazem. Am I correct in assuming that
          without the device or part of it, and without
          the pilot, it will be impossible for Doctor
          Krebbs to accomplish anything?

                    SCHARFF
          You are correct.

                    MINISTER
          But Marcus _can_ duplicate his work.

                    SCHARFF
          Of course. But even _he_ will not know _why_ his
          equipment malfunctioned, _why_ the plane
          carrying it crashed - until he can talk to
          the pilot. That is essential.

                    MINISTER
          Then we must see to it that he does not do
          so, mustn't we, my dear Scharff?

He stands up; Scharff at once gets to his feet.

                    SCHARFF
          Of course, _Cedi_ Minister.

Without another word nor glance the Minister leaves. Scharff stands staring after him, then he sits down. He picks up the phone and jiggles the cradle.

                    SCHARFF
          Richter. Get me Kahill. At once...Abu Ali!
          Here are the orders to be transmitted to the
          agents in the field at once...Effective
          immediately, your target is to be
          eliminated...I repeat -- _kill your target_!

                                                    CUT TO:

EXT. HILLS - DUSK

Tom is slowly making his way down a broad, eroded depression between two humpbacked hills. He is exhausted and parched with thirst.

EXT. RIDGE - FIELD GLASSES

CAMERA PULLS BACK to reveal a man lying on ridge, observing the far hills. It is the Artist, encountered by Gordon. He looks appraisingly at the setting sun, then resumes his watch. CAMERA PANS to a rifle with a scope, leaning against a rock outcropping, out of the sun and safe from the sandy dirt, then back to the Artist, watching.

BINOCULAR SHOT - ARTIST'S POV - Tom as he is coming closer.

ANGLE ON ARTIST, watching. Suddenly a VOICE is heard O.S.

                    VOICE (O.S.)
          Are you all right, sir?

The Artist whirls around - between him and his rifle stands Ranger Adams.

                         ADAMS
               Is everything all right? Can I be of help?

The Artist stands up.

                         ARTIST
               No. No, thank you. I - I was just admiring
               the mountains in the sunset.

                         ADAMS
               It can be quite a spectacular sight.
                         (nods toward the gun)
               I see you have a gun with you. Hunting is
               strictly forbidden within the confines of the
               National Park. Firearms are not allowed.

                         ARTIST
               I - I didn't intend to shoot anything, man.
               I - well, I just get a kick outta sighting in
               on a wild burro, you know. Or something...It
               isn't even loaded.

Ingenuously he moves toward the gun. Adams stops him.

                         ADAMS
               That's all right, sir. I'll take it.

He picks up the rifle; he works the bolt; a round jumps out from
the breach and plops on the sand. Adams picks it up.

                         ADAMS
               Perhaps you'd better come with me, sir.

                         ARTIST
               Where to?

                         ADAMS
               Ranger Headquarters. I think it would be
               better if the Chief had a word with you.

The Artist looks at Adams with a calculating narrowing of the
eyes, as they start down the precarious slope, the Artist in the
lead. Below on the road, his dune buggy can be seen, with the
ranger truck drawn up behind it...They are halfway down the slope
when suddenly the Artist loses his footing; he goes tumbling
down; he tries to get up - and falls back in pain.

                         ARTIST
               Oh, shit, man!

He begins to rub his knee just above his <u>heavy boot</u>. Adams comes
up to him.

                         ADAMS
               Are you badly hurt?

                         ARTIST
          It's my knee. I - I hope to hell it's just
          twisted.

Adams bends down to look at it. Instantly the Artist explodes
into action. With all his power, he jabs a knife, drawn from his
boot, up into the chest of the ranger, twisting it. Adams falls
across his killer's legs; blood soaks the pants and is sucked up
by the thirsty ground...The Artist rolls out from under the body;
his pants are soaked with blood. He switches pants with the body
exchanging pocket contents; he looks around. Nearby is a small
fissure under an overhanging rock. He carries Adams to it and
pushes him in under the rock. He picks up his blood-soaked pants
and stuffs them in after. He has a sudden thought; he pulls the
pants out, finds Adams' wallet and empties it of cash. Stuffing
everything back in he conceals the opening with rocks...He picks
up his gun and puts it in the buggy; he rummages around in the
ranger truck and comes up with a length of rope. He hitches the
two vehicles together and begins to tow the ranger truck away...

EXT. CANYON - DUSK

The Artist, towing the truck, comes to a halt. He goes back to
the truck, again rummaging around. He comes up with a large
rusty nail, and a jack; he puts the jack in his buggy and uses
the nail to let the air out of the truck's spare tire...

He bends down at the rear right tire and paces the nail,
standing, in front of it - leaning its tip against the rubber...
He gets into his buggy - and eases the two vehicles forward.

CLOSE-UP - NAIL as it is driven into the tire - which begins to
go flat.

ANGLE ON ARTIST as he unhitches the truck, gets back into his
buggy and drives off.

                                                       CUT TO:

EXT. NIGHT SKY WITH FULL MOON

The distant whop-whop-whop SOUND of a helicopter can be heard
approaching - and presently a chopper flies across the luminous
disc of the moon.

INT. NIGHT RECONNAISSANCE HELICOPTER

The big HH53H helicopter is equipped with the newest Night
Tracking System; a PILOT and a CO-PILOT are watching the video
display screens in front of them.

THE GROUND as seen through the equipment. It looks eerily red,
totally alien.

HELICOPTER - flying over the rocky terrain. A PARA-RESCUE
JUMPER can be seen hanging out of the door on his safety straps -
watching...

INT. HELICOPTER - SCREEN

The weird landscape passes by below...Suddenly there is movement - hardly noticeable.

CLOSE SHOT - P.J. IN DOOR. With his Night Vision Goggles he looks like a visitor from outer space, ogling Mother Earth.

                            P.J.
     Sir. I think I saw something move. Three
     o'clock. Two hundred yards.

The chopper veers right.

INT. HELICOPTER - SCREEN

Nothing moves. The pilot and co-pilot are watching and working the equipment.

CLOSE SHOT - SCREEN. Half concealed among the rocks below a figure moves - looking eerily red; it cannot be identified.

INT. HELICOPTER

                          CO-PILOT
     There! Two o'clock...

The Pilot makes a course correction; both men watch the screen intently.

CLOSE SHOT - SCREEN. From a rock formation a form suddenly bolts from cover. It is a small wild burro; it runs off in panic.

                            PILOT
     Shit! Just a wild ass.

EXT. HELICOPTER - NIGHT

As it flies off.

EXT. ROCKY TERRAIN NEAR VALLEY

Tom is warily making his way among the rocks. In the distance the whop-whop-whop of the approaching chopper can be heard. Tom looks up apprehensively.

CHOPPER DOOR. A P.J. is scanning the ground below through his sci-fi-looking N.V. Goggles.

EXT. ROCKS - ANGLE ON TOM

He runs for cover.

INT. HELICOPTER

Flying over the terrain, observing.

POV HELICOPTER. The eerie, red, alien-looking landscape passes below.

> P.J.
> (over intercom)
> Movement, sir...I think...Seven o'clock. Four hundred yards.

EXT. HELICOPTER

It wheels around, low over the rocks.

EXT. GROUND - ANGLE ON TOM

He squeezes himself under a rock formation.

INT. HELICOPTER

It comes up on the area.

CLOSE SHOT - SCREEN. The unearthly, rocky slope passes by below. There is nothing to be seen.

> PILOT
> Nothing! Let's try the next sector.

EXT. THE HELICOPTER - NIGHT

It flies off.

EXT. GROUND - TOM

He emerges from his hiding place and moves off, down the slope...

DISSOLVE TO:

EXT. INDIAN VILLAGE - ESTABLISHING SHOT - NIGHT

All is quiet.

EXT. THE CORRAL

A few horses are standing near the water trough.

EXT. THE DESERT

Tom is cautiously creeping along the wash of an arroyo. In the b.g. we can make out the Indian village; the corral; and the tall palm trees of the man-made oasis. Tom stops; he is terribly thirsty; his nostrils dilate as the smell of water reaches him; he crawls on - OUT OF FRAME.

EXT. THE CORRAL

A couple of horses are drinking at the trough, suddenly they lift their heads and look off anxiously; they snort uneasily. Tom is creeping toward the water trough. Tom scrambles to the trough an submerges his face in the water. The horses SNORT in protest.

INT. INDIAN ADOBE HUT

It is the shack of two INDIAN WRANGLERS; there are a couple of bunks and a crude table and chairs. On the wall hang various pieces of harnessing; also an old double-barrelled shotgun. From outside come the SOUNDS made by the uneasy horses. The two Indians look at each other; then one of them glances toward the shotgun on the wall; the other grins. The first Indian gets up; takes down the shotgun; checks that both barrels are loaded, and goes to the door - opens it.

EXT. OUTSIDE ADOBE HUT

The door opens; silently the Indian steps out.

ANGLE - THE TROUGH AT THE CORRAL. Tom is drinking; he lifts his head; he listens intently, trying to make out something over the NOISE made by the horses. Silently he slips away from the trough and crawls toward the brush.

ANGLE - ACROSS INDIAN IN F.G. - TO CORRAL TROUGH IN B.G. In the distance, a half-hidden form slips quietly away from the trough and steals toward the brush. The Indian raises his gun.

SHOT ALONG THE GUN BARREL TO THE TROUGH AREA. Again the shadowy form moves; with a deafening ROAR the Indian's gun goes off.

ANGLE ON TOM. He is crouched on all fours; a handful of buckshot slams into his shoulder. With a snarl Tom grabs at the wound then scampers away into the bushes.

ANGLE ON THE INDIAN. Again he raises his gun.

											CUT TO:

EXT. OUTSIDE RANGER HEADQUARTERS - NIGHT

Paul and Randi are standing at the entrance; Randi looks up in alarm.

				RANDI
		What was that?

				PAUL
				(pointing)
		Came from that direction.

                    RANDI
          Over by the stables?

                    PAUL
          One of the boys must be taking potshots at a
          bobcat.

                    RANDI
          Bobcats? Down here?

                    PAUL
          They come down from the mountains now and
          again - in the cool of the night.

                    RANDI
          Goodnight, Paul. I'm going back to the
          cabin. I feel so - so restless.

                    PAUL
          You don't want me to drive you down?

                    RANDI
          No...Please. I'll walk. The air'll do me
          good.

                    PAUL
          We'll finish mapping out the search areas for
          tomorrow. Goodnight, Randi.

                    RANDI
          Goodnight, Paul...Don't forget. I want to go
          with you.

She walks off hurriedly.

EXT. ROAD NEAR FURNACE CREEK RANCH

Randi comes walking down the deserted road; she is in deep
thought; off the road we see the palm grove; Randi stops at the
trees. She looks up into the sky; her eyes are bright with
unshed tears; she stands motionless.

REVERSE ANGLE - ACROSS RANDI TO THE TOP OF THE PALMS AND THE HIGH
MOON. She stands facing the palm grove and the bright moon.

CLOSE - RANDI. She looks comforted, serene - but her eyes are
still bright. She turns and walks toward the ranch - OUT OF
FRAME

EXT. FURNACE CREEK RANCH

It is near the Outdoor Museum; Randi comes walking toward the
museum gate. She decides to take the short-cut and walks into
the museum grounds.

EXT. FURNACE CREEK RANCH OUTDOOR MUSEUM

The moonlight streams through the mosaic forms of the old mining equipment pieces standing in the museum area. Giant 20-mule team wagons, heavy and high-wheeled, lord it over crushers, drillers, ore carts and pumps. The eerie indistinctness of the moonlight lends a strange aura of menace to the scene. Randi comes walking along the path. She follows the trail around the huge wagon; she looks preoccupied.

ANOTHER ANGLE ON RANDI. Only her FOOTSTEPS crunching the gravel can be heard. All at once the sharp CLANK of iron against iron comes from the deepest shadows ahead of her. She stops. She looks suddenly scared. Slowly she walks on - toward the shadows ahead; each footstep can be heard distinctly in the still of the night.

MED. WALKING - RANDI'S POV. Randi (CAMERA) is walking on; we HEAR the footsteps - and her BREATHING. Nearer and nearer toward a huge ore crusher looming tall walks the girl. Suddenly, a figure jumps out from behind the iron hiding place - into a FULL CLOSE-UP!...It is Tom. He looks terrifying; the blood from his cracked skull is matted in his hair; his eyes are wild; his teeth bared in a snarl; the shotgun wound in his shoulder and the torn cloth around it are bloody; he looks like a dangerous, wounded animal. There is a short, startled SCREAM from Randi, O.S.

ANOTHER ANGLE - TWO SHOT. With a low growl, Tom springs upon Randi, clawing at her, ripping her thin blouse at the shoulder. There is a choked, shocked outcry from the girl.

                    RANDI
          Tom!

And she falls to the ground...Poised over her - alert and menacing - is Tom. His face is wild and tense; his fingers clawed, as he watches the motionless woman. She doesn't stir. Slowly, gradually, the terror-fury leaves Tom; he relaxes and watches the woman with growing curiosity.

CLOSE-UP - RANDI. She is horror-stricken.

ANGLE ON TOM AND RANDI. He is looking absorbedly down upon the woman; his face subtly changes expression; this is the male animal scenting the presence of - a female...Randi stares directly up into her husband's almost unrecognizable face. She opens her mouth and starts to cry out. Tom quickly clamps a grimy, scarred hand over her mouth. Her eyes stare large and frightened above Tom's hand. Slowly she relaxes - and Tom's hand is withdrawn. Randi sits up; the two of them regard each other for a moment; Tom with frank curiosity - but without any recognition whatsoever; Randi with a mixture of growing horror and desperation as she really sees her husband. Suddenly there is the NOISE of a screen door being slammed. Tom immediately stiffens and faces the sound with alert tension.

> MAN'S VOICE (O.S.)
> Good night, Frank...

Tom is listening - hard.

> MAN'S VOICE (O.S.)
> See you tomorrow...

Crunching, heavy FOOTSTEPS are heard.

> ANOTHER MAN'S VOICE (O.S.)
> Good night!

Tom shrinks back from the approaching FOOTSTEPS; he turns to run - almost immediately whirls back upon Randi; he grabs her and hauls her with him; they run silently away among the distorted shadows of the old museum pieces. Randi wanting to cry out, but not daring to do so...

CUT TO:

EXT. FURNACE CREEK RANCH PALM GROVE - NIGHT

The trees stand tall and straight, waving their huge fronds far above. Tom and Randi come running through the grove - until they disappear; he is pulling her along. They start out into the desert.

EXT. DEVIL'S CORN FIELD

Tom is walking at a fast clip through the weird arrow-weed clumps; Randi trails behind him, occasionally breaking into a half-run to keep up.

VEGETATED DUNE. A lonely hillock dune with sparse vegetation growing on it like a scraggly crown. Tom and Randi approach and start to crawl up into the scrub brush.

THE DUNE. Tom and Randi are crawling in among the weeds and shrubs clinging to the little dune; they settle down in a small sand hollow - and regard each other solemnly for a while. Randi is obviously frightened.

> RANDI
> Tom...?

Tom regards the girl solemnly and with fascination; but also without the slightest hint of comprehension or recognition.

> RANDI
> Tom...Look at me! It's Randi...Tom,
> Please...Please know me...Tom...

Randi looks searchingly and pleadingly at her husband; he looks at her curiously, but there is no response. Slowly she lowers her head.

CAMERA PANS UP - AWAY from the two people - to peer through the shrubbery, up into the starry sky, with the bright full moon.

DISSOLVE TO:

EXT. SUNRISE SHOT AT SCENIC POINT IN DEATH VALLEY - SUNRISE

EXT. RANGER HEADQUARTERS

It is early morning.

INT. RANGER HEADQUARTERS

Paul is sitting at the desk talking heatedly on the telephone. Ward, Stark and Trafford are listening to him.

> PAUL
> ...There's no doubt, Colonel...he was shot by one of the wranglers...No, I don't know how serious it is...
> (his impatience grows)
> She must be with him. Why else would she be missing?

He is controlling his mounting anger with difficulty.

> PAUL
> All right, sir, I will take the responsibility. But I must also insist on a full-scale search. There is no...
> (cut off, he listens)
> In one hour?...Right...
> (he hangs up, not too gently)
> Damn his hide!

> WARD
> What'd he say?

> PAUL
> He's sending half a dozen more choppers.

> WARD
> That's something, at least.

> PAUL
> But far from enough. He's also trying to arrange for an SR-71 photo overflight.

> WARD
> You know what beats me? How does Tom keep evading all the top technology we can throw at him. One lone guy.

                    PAUL
               (grimly)
          He's got one hell of an ally.

                    WARD
          Ally? Who?

                    PAUL
          Death Valley.

                    WARD
               (he nods)
          We _are_ running out of time.

                    PAUL
               (he turns to Stark)
          Any word about Adams?

                    STARK
          No. We found his truck. Flat tire. And he'd
          gone out without a jack. He should have
          known better...

                    PAUL
          Any ideas where he could be?

                    STARK
          None. His truck was found way off his
          assigned sector.

                    PAUL
          What the hell _is_ going on out there?

                    WARD
          Paul. You - you don't think he could have
          run into Tom?

                    PAUL
          I - don't know, Quent. This thing keeps
          getting more complicated all the time. First
          Tom. Then Adams. And now - Randi.

                    WARD
          Could she have gone with him - voluntarily?
          In an effort to help?

                    PAUL
          No. I am certain she did not. Remember.
          There _was_ a struggle. We saw the signs.
               (he turns to Trafford)
          Why would Tom - take her along?

                                                  CUT TO:

EXT. VEGETATED DUNE - DAY

It looks quiet and peaceful.

ANGLE ON TOM AND RANDI huddled in the hidden hollow under the bushes; they are regarding one another; Randi with a mixture of fear and concern; Tom with uncomprehending curiosity.

                    RANDI
    Tom...Tom...I - I know you don't understand
    my words...but - I want to help you.

She looks at Tom with compassion - but she is obviously frightened.

                    RANDI
    You're confused...afraid...I understand.

Tom watches her; he makes a sudden movement toward his injured shoulder; through the torn cloth and the wound can be seen; he scratches at it with a dirty hand. Randi sees it --

                    RANDI
    Oh, my God! It was _you_ they shot at! How
    frightened you must have been.

She brings out a handkerchief; slowly she reaches her hand toward Tom; he draws back at once, growling suspicious, alarmed. Randi - though frightened - gently persists.

                    RANDI
    It's all right...It's all right.

Tom looks confused; absentmindedly he touches the spot of caked blood on top of his head.

                    RANDI
    Be still - Tom...It's all right...

She slowly reaches for Tom's shoulder; he shrinks back - but lets her touch the wound; he winces - but keeps watching her.

                    RANDI
    There..you see? It's all right.

Carefully she begins to remove the torn cloth around the wound.

                    RANDI
    The buckshot're still there!

She starts to pick the buckshot from Tom's injury. He lets her work - watching her warily, but instinctively knowing that she is helping him. She speaks soothingly to him...

                         RANDI
            Easy now...Be still...It's all right...I
            won't leave you...I'll stay with you...Get
            help...You won't have to run away anymore...

She finishes; she places the handkerchief inside Tom's torn suit
to protect the wound. He is looking at her with curiosity and
growing interest...Suddenly he stiffens; carefully he turns his
head and looks intently at the surrounding vegetation.

CLOSE SHOT - LARGE LIZARD sitting in the sand under the weed.

TWO SHOT. Both Tom and Randi are watching the lizard. Tom
reaches for it and it quickly moves out of the way...Again he
tries to pick the lizard up; again it moves. Randi is watching
Tom's efforts; he gets a determined expression on his face;
suddenly he throws himself lightning fast toward the lizard -
hands outstretched...He grabs the big lizard and drags it back
from its attempted escape, wriggling frantically in his grip...

ANOTHER ANGLE ON TOM AND RANDI. Suddenly Tom makes a wrenching
movement with his hands - breaking the lizard's back; Randi's
face freezes in terror; Tom raises the dead lizard to his mouth -
and with his teeth he tears into the skin; Randi is on the verge
of becoming ill with revulsion; she looks nauseated, horrified;
Tom rips the skin off the reptile and tears a strip of bloody
meat from it with his fingers; he holds it up toward Randi.

(NOTE: The action takes place OUT OF SIGHT OF CAMERA hidden by
Tom's body. We follow it through Tom's movements and Randi's
reactions. Not until Tom holds out the meat do we see anything.)

Randi makes a tremendous effort not to get sick; slowly she
regains control; she puts the back of her hand over her mouth in
a gesture of refusal. Tom looks puzzled; then - unconcerned he
pops the bloody lizard meat into his mouth. Randi is watching
him with revulsion...and with growing realization of his true
state of mind...All of a sudden the NOISE of an approaching
vehicle intrudes upon their awareness. At once Tom falls to the
ground - pulling Randi down with him; they watch from between the
shrubs.

EXT. DESERT ROAD

On the road going past the sand dune, a dune buggy is approaching
from the distance, its muffler noisy. The driver is looking
around; it is the Artist.

                         RANDI
            Tom. Here comes someone. They will help.

Tom looks apprehensive. He is watching the vehicle with fear and
hatred. As the buggy comes nearer, Randi gets increasingly
excited. Suddenly she waves and calls, trying to get up. At
                                                    CONTINUED:

CONTINUED:

once Tom grabs her - and pulls her down roughly, holding her, "protecting" her from the pursuing "monster," he has come to know and fear.

ANGLE ON BUGGY with the Artist as it is passing by - disappearing down the road.

ON TOM AND RANDI. Tom set Randi free; he scowls at her, puzzled, angry; she looks frightened, defeated; roughly he pulls her to her feet and pushes her before him, off the dune toward the desert floor.

THE DUNE. Tom and Randi emerge from the bush - Randi stops in dismay. She stares straight ahead - dread and awe in her face; she turns toward Tom as if in disbelief; then looks ahead again.

                    RANDI
No, Tom. Not out there. We'll never make it.

LONG POV SHOT - THE SAND DUNES OF DEATH VALLEY. The vast panorama of naked, wind-sculptured sand hills stretches its expanse as far as they eye can see. From directly overhead, the sun beats down.

                    RANDI
How can I make you understand?

She regards Tom pleadingly; anxiously he looks back toward the road and prods her to go on; the two of them start across the sand dunes.

                              CUT TO:

INT. AIR RECONNAISSANCE PHOTO ANALYSIS LAB - ESTABLISHING - DAY

It is a large, impressive room with intricate and complicated equipment to receive, project and analyze relayed photographs. Military personnel and technicians are at work; appropriate ad lib technical jargon in b.g.

CLOSER ANGLE. OFFICER ON PHONE.

                    OFFICER
Yes, General Ryan, an SR-71 _would_ be available, but -
          (he listens; frowns)
I'll transfer you to Colonel Porter, Sir.

CLOSE SHOT. COLONEL PORTER - sitting at a desk overlooking the whole area. The phone at his side rings; he picks it up.

                    PORTER
          Porter...Yes, General...Yes, it can be done -
          but a photographic mission of that sort is
          not -
                    (he listens; frowns)
          I'll have to get Pentagon clearance...Yes,
          Sir. I'll get on it at once...

He hangs up...He picks up the red phone...

                                                  CUT TO:

ANGLE ON THE SUN blazing in the sky.

ON TOM AND RANDI as they toil across the sand, hot and spent.
Tom stops; looks around; Randi staggers up to him and looks down
on the sand - exhausted; Tom squints up at the sun; the sweat is
rolling down his forehead and face.

                                                  CUT TO:

EXT. SIDE ROAD IN THE VALLEY - CANVAS WATER BAG - DAY

Moist cool droplets have formed on the surface and are trickling
down the porous canvas. The bag is hanging on the side of a
parked Scout. CAMERA PANS to Paul and Hays who stand before the
Scout consulting a map, spread out on the hood; they both look up
at the SOUND of an approaching vehicle...Ward's Scout, with
Wilson driving, comes up the road to join the others; Ward and
Wilson get out; Ward has a map in his hand; he goes over to Paul;
Wilson ambles up to Hays. CAMERA MOVES TO ANGLE ON HAYS AND
WILSON.

                    WILSON
          Say, Sarge...We've been all over this mother-
          forsaken place...Where are we now?

Hays points to the map.

                    HAYS
          Right...there.

                    WILSON
                    (reading)
          Death Valley...Funeral Mountains...Coffin
          Canyon.

He looks up at Hays and shrugs his shoulders.

                    WILSON
          So - who's superstitious!

                    HAYS
          Glad you like it here...Looks like we'll be
          here a while.

                    WILSON
          Just don't go putting me on no <u>graveyard</u>
          shift, Sarge!

Hays groans. Wilson goes for the water bag. He takes out his
canteen cup; fills it with water from the water bag and drinks
long and deep; he throws the rest of the water on the sandy
ground. CAMERA PANS this action; the dry sand sucks up the
moisture instantly.

                                                    CUT TO:

EXT. SAND DUNES - ANGLE ON TOM AND RANDI - AFTERNOON

Tom is racked with thirst; his parched mouth and throat work in
an effort to swallow imaginary moisture. He and Randi are
reaching the crest of a large dune; as they do, Tom turns
excitedly to Randi; he tugs at her, then runs down the steep
slope of the dune; after only a second's hesitation, Randi
follows him - disappearing over the crest.

EXT. BADWATER - AFTERNOON

The pools of clear water look inviting and refreshing. Tom comes
running into the scene - followed at some distance by Randi. He
runs to the water and falls to the ground. Eagerly he dips his
head into the water -- and takes a deep draft. Immediately he
spits out the water and coughs. He sits up; staring at the water
dully; Randi comes hobbling up; she sinks to her knees, cups her
hands scooping water up to her mouth; suddenly Tom notices her -
at once he hits her hands, making her spill the water. She looks
shocked. Tom tries to convey to Randi that the water is bad; he
wipes his mouth hard with his hand - and spits. Gingerly Randi
test the water; it is salt. Her faces takes on the first hint of
trust. Tom gets up, takes hold of her - and drags her to her
feet - away from the water. CAMERA FOLLOWS them and HOLDS ON a
sign; it reads:

                         <u>BADWATER</u>
                    280 FEET BELOW SEA LEVEL
                    IN THIS AREA IS THE LOWEST
                  LAND IN THE WESTERN HEMISPHERE

                                                    CUT TO:

INT. AIR RECONNAISSANCE PHOTO LAB - DAY

Operators are projecting and examining a series of photographs.
Colonel Porter is present. An exposure of a large, wild-looking
area of the valley, taken at high altitude, is being projected.

                    PORTER
          Hold that.

With a flashlight pointer he indicates an area.

                    PORTER
          Enlarge that.

The picture is enlarged. Two tiny figures can be made out...
Again the photo is enlarged. The figures are Tom and Randi.

                    PORTER
          Time.

At once the time the exposure was made is flashed in a corner of
the screen - blinking on and off: 16:17

                    PORTER
          Give me the next exposure. Overlay.

Over the projected photo a second exposure is superimposed. The
two figures are further along. The time 16:22 flashes. An
operator projects a line from the first position of the figures
to the second - and ahead. The line points toward the wild,
rugged expanse. A ground coordinate grid is superimposed over
the photos. Porter picks up a phone.

                    PORTER
          Priority message to Captain Jarman: Subjects
          spotted. As of 16:22 hours headed for grid
          coordinates P-47 - M-62...the area known as
          the Devil's Golf Course...

                                                       CUT TO:

EXT. DEVIL'S GOLF COURSE - AFTERNOON

The beginning of the rugged area of crusted mud and salt...On the
adjoining dirt road, two Scouts, a ranger truck and a jeep stop.
Paul gets out of one Scout, in which sits Hays; Ward dismounts
from the other, leaving Wilson in the vehicle. The two officers
walk to the ranger truck and confer with a ranger; from the jeep,
Gordon joins them...Suddenly there is the distant SOUND of
whirling helicopter rotors. The men look up.

ANGLE ON HELICOPTER flying low over the salt flats quite far out;
the aircraft makes an abrupt turn.

THE ROAD. The men are watching the helicopter. In b.g. the
Scouts can be seen. Hays is talking on his radio. Suddenly he
calls:

                    HAYS
          They've spotted them!

The men at once run toward the Scout; Hays points.

                    HAYS
          Crossing the salt flats.

He picks up the field glasses and looks through them. Then men come up to the Scout; Hays hands the field glasses to Paul.

                    PAUL

    Where?

                    HAYS

    Almost across.

Paul scans the horizon with the binoculars.

                    RADIO

    Armadillo One...this is Skybird Three.

                    HAYS

    Go ahead, Skybird Three.

                    RADIO

    Returning to base. Low on fuel...

INT. HELICOPTER

ANGLE ON HELICOPTER looking down.

                    PILOT

    Can't land on those damned salt crags.
    They're sharp as spikes.

THE ROAD. The men are listening to the radio.

                    RADIO

    Got 'em spotted for you...Hope you get them.
    Out.

                    HAYS

    Roger, Skybird. Out.

Paul again scans the flats with his binoculars.

BINOCULAR SHOT as they sweep the salt flats, across the sharp pinnacles. Suddenly two small figures come into view, stumbling across the jagged, knife-edged ridges.

                    PAUL (O.S.)

    There they are!

Caught in the binoculars, Tom and Randi are struggling across the crags. Both are bruised and limping...

THE ROAD. The men are straining to look. Paul turns to Hays.

                    PAUL

    Contact the other choppers.

                              HAYS
                    Yes, sir.

He begins to make contact; Paul turns to Gordon.

                              PAUL
                    Can we get to them?

                              GORDON
                    Not much of a chance...We can't <u>drive</u>
                    across...We'll have to go around...By the
                    time we do - they'll be in the mountains.

Wilson is standing at the edge of the flats next to the ranger jeep; suddenly he calls.

                              WILSON
                    Sir! There's a path here! Across the flats.
                    I can head them off...

He jumps into the jeep, starts up and takes off down toward the salt flats.

                              GORDON
                    Wait! It only goes a little ways!

                              PAUL
                    Wilson!

But the jeep careens down the rugged path in a cloud of dust.

                              PAUL
                    Wilson! Come back!

ANGLE ON JEEP bouncing along the rocky trail. Wilson has trouble keeping the vehicle under control.

ANGLE FROM JEEP across the hood to the crusted salt peaks racing by. The vehicle lurches and bounces.

ANGLE ON WILSON. He is sweating; he looks a little scared now, but still determined.

THE MEN anxiously watching the careening jeep.

ON THE JEEP. The going is getting more and more difficult. Steel-hard salt-and-mud rocks litter the narrow trail. Wilson is bouncing in the seat, keeping the jeep on the trail with difficulty. Suddenly the trail ends abruptly; the front wheel of the jeep hits a large boulder with a jarring impact and bounces into the air. Wilson is thrown from his seat; out of the jeep, which careens off the trail into the sharp salt peaks. Wilson's foot is caught between the seat and the side of the jeep; he is being dragged across the razor sharp crags. The jeep's momentum
                                                        CONTINUED:

CONTINUED:

only carries it about twenty feet - but it is enough to cut the heavy-duty tires literally to ribbons and they EXPLODE in loud blow-outs before the jeep comes to a halt, wedged in the salt rocks.

THE MEN as they race toward the trail and the jeep in horror.

PANNING SHOT - JEEP. From a CLOSE SHOT of mangled tire, CAMERA PANS to a QUICK FULL SHOT of Wilson. His leg is still caught in the jeep; he lies across the jagged salt spikes; his jacket is bunched up around his chest; his arms are flung their full length over his head as he was dragged across the knife-edge crags. He is horribly gashed. He is dead.

ANOTHER ANGLE - THE JEEP wedged at a crazy angle in the salt peaks; the outflung arms of Wilson can be seen sticking out from behind the jeep on its far side. Paul, Ward, Hays and the rangers come running up to the jeep; they stop short and look in horror at the remains of Wilson on the other side.

ANGLE ON PAUL. He looks grim; he turns from the body and starts to walk away. CAMERA PANS to the nearby mountains - and ZOOMS IN. Among the craggy rocks a man can be seen crouched among the rocks.

ANGLE ON MAN. It is the Artist. With binoculars, he is observing the scene below. He lifts the binoculars to a view of the salt flats.

ANGLE ON TOM AND RANDI stumbling across the salt peaks; Randi falters, loses her footing on the treacherous crags and falls to one knee. She looks up at Tom - tears in her eyes; she is exhausted, hurt; she regards her husband with a pleading look.

                    RANDI
     Tom...I...can't...

Her head sinks down. Tom, too, is dead tired. He is about to go on; suddenly his face distorts in pain; absentmindedly he touches the spot on his head, where the caked blood can be seen. He looks toward Randi. He slowly walks over to her, lifts her up and begins to walk toward the mountains, supporting her...

                                        DISSOLVE TO:

EXT. DESERT MOUNTAINS - DUSK

Tom and Randi are slowly making their way up into the mountains. They are spent, battered and thirsty. Tom is a little ahead of Randi; he comes to a rock outcropping; he looks around - and suddenly runs forward.

EXT. HOLE-IN-THE-WALL SPRING - DUSK

The water is trickling down from the little spring. Tom comes running into PICTURE; he begins to lap up the clear water. Randi joins him - and he makes room for her. They are quenching their thirst; then they sink down on the ground to rest. Randi takes out a handkerchief; she wets it - and wipes her burning face. Tom gets up and crawls back a short distance - looking out over the salt flats. CAMERA PANS with him.

ANGLE ON RANDI. She is hot and perspiring; she runs the cool, moist cloth around her neck; she unbuttons a button on her torn and dirty blouse - then looks toward her husband.

RANDI'S POV - TOM. He has his back to her, crouched at some rocks, looking out over the valley.

ANGLE ON RANDI as she unbuttons another button; she turns her back and opens her blouse; with the handkerchief she begins to give herself a cooling sponge bath; she glances in Tom's direction.

ANGLE ON TOM AND RANDI. Tom is watching the woman intently; curiosity, interest and desire are building in his eyes. He moves toward her. Randi offers him the handkerchief.

>   RANDI
>   Here, Tom...It'll feel good.

Tom is paying no attention to her words; his eyes are fixed on the open blouse. He reaches out and touches her. Randi pulls back, startled.

>   RANDI
>   Tom...!

Tom is not hearing the words - he knows only the sudden urgent feeling in his loins; he has no thought of resisting it. He moves toward his wife and begins to pull at her blouse; he suddenly buries his face in her breasts, his hands frantically pulling her body to him. Randi is terrified.

>   RANDI
>   Tom! Don't..Don't...

She cringes backward over the rocks as he moves after her. He grabs her and they both crash to the ground.

>   RANDI
>   (badly frightened)
>   Please! Tom! No!...No!...Not like this...

Tom, intent only on his wants, is on top of her, pressing against her, tearing at her clothing - and his own...Randi, struggling under his weight, is trapped beneath him. He rips apart the snap on her pants and begins to tug them down - oblivious to a faint,

CONTINUED:

CONTINUED:

growing DRONE...With a sudden, shocking ROAR, a helicopter hurtles low across them, shooting out from behind the mountain range. Instantly Tom rolls off Randi; she pulls her clothing around her; he grabs her and pulls her down between the rocks.

ANGLE FROM GROUND - U.S.A.F. HELICOPTER IN FLIGHT

INT. HELICOPTER - DUSK. ANGLE ON PILOT. He is looking down; he is obviously not discovering the two people hidden below.

HELICOPTER'S POV. The barren, rocky desert mountains below are apparently deserted; not a thing is stirring.

FROM GROUND - THE HELICOPTER is flying off.

ANGLE ON TOM AND RANDI. Tom peers out between the rocks; he looks back over his shoulder at Randi; she is just finishing buttoning the last button on her blouse and gathering her torn clothing around her. He looks back in the direction of the valley from where they came; a frown of worry clouds his face. He gets up and pulls the shaken Randi to her feet; he begins to walk away; Randi has no choice but to follow him. They leave FRAME...

CUT TO:

EXT. WILDROSE CANYON - DUSK

It is the crest of a hill; on the slope grow scattered scrub pines and shrubs. Tom and Randi appear over the crest. They are dead tired; suddenly Tom stops - and looks intently ahead, down the slope.

TOM'S POV OF CHARCOAL KILNS. At the bottom of the little valley below stands a row of curious large, cone-shaped stone structures, looking like giant rock beehives. They are abandoned charcoal kilns from bygone mining days.

CHARCOAL KILNS. Tom and Randi come into the scene; they look down the row of stone hives with curiosity; they walk to the nearest one; Tom peers inside, Randi sinks down and leans against the rough wall. Tom joins her. The two exhausted people are resting on the ground against the wall of the kiln. Tom looks around; his interest is caught by something he sees.

TOM'S POV - BUSH as a large bird circling over it lands and disappears into the thicket of the branches.

ANGLE ON RANDI AND TOM as Tom slowly gets up; Randi is watching. Tom walks toward the bush...The bird suddenly appears and takes off. Tom walks up to the bush; he parts the branches.

CLOSE SHOT - BIRD NEST resting in the branches; there are four fair-sized eggs in it.

THE KILNS - ANGLE ON RANDI waiting for Tom; he appears - holding the eggs in his hand; he squats next to Randi and places the eggs on the ground between them. He picks up one egg; he crushes it in the palm of his hand; it is fresh - the yolk and white run between his fingers; he puts his hand to his mouth and licks it. Randi reaches for one of the eggs; instantly Tom stiffens; watching him, she picks it up; there is a moment's tension - and Tom accepts her action and returns to eating. Randi searches for and finds a small stick; with it she pokes two holes in the ends of the egg; she looks at it for a moment in indecision - then sucks out the nourishment. She eats the rest of the eggs. Tom sits watching her; he licks the gashes on his hands - much like a dog or cat might lick its wounds. Randi finishes the last egg; she looks sadly at her husband.

        RANDI
 Thank you...Tom.

Tom gets up; he pulls Randi to her feet; together they walk to the nearest kiln and enter.

INT. KILN

Tom and Randi come in through the opening; the kiln is quite dark; high on the back wall a small, half-moon shaped window opening is set; a few old scorched timbers lean against the wall; the flooring is sand and charcoal ashes. Tom and Randi sink down on the floor; Randi leans against the wall - and they look at one another. Tom again absentmindedly touches the spot of caked blood high on his head; he face contorts as if in a great effort to...to...But they are both exhausted, spent - and they fall into a deep sleep.

        DISSOLVE TO:

SAME LOCATION - NIGHT

Tom is tossing in his sleep, moaning. Randi wakes and gazes over at him - compassion and hurt in her eyes as she watches this poor, tortured creature that is her husband...Tom lets out a small cry and rolls over in his sleep toward Randi. Randi stiffens as his arm falls across her legs and his head comes to rest in her lap. Then - slowly - she relaxes as she looks down at her sleeping husband, and she strokes his hair. Two large tears glisten in her eyes; she whisper softly:

        RANDI
 Please...let them find us soon...Anyone...

        CUT TO:

INT. BAGHDAD - SCHARFF'S OFFICE - NIGHT

CLOSE SHOT PAD lying on desk. A hand is doodling on a misshapen drawing of a rocket or guided missile; the thing is squat and ugly - a scud.

>SCHARFF (O.S.)
>Yes, Cedi Minister, I fully understand...

CAMERA WIDENS to see Scharff sitting at his desk, his face glistens with the sweat of acute discomfort.

>SCHARFF
>...Fully...Yes, I...
>>(listens; wets his lips)
>Yes, Cedi Minister, of course I shall person- ally guarantee that the order is carried out...But I should like respectfully to point out --

There is a CLICK as the phone is being disconnected. For a moment Scharff stares at the dead phone; then he jiggles the cradle.

>SCHARFF
>Richter. Get Kahlil and get in here. Now!

He slams the receiver down. He starts on his doodle - adding billows of angry black smoke to the rocket. He presses the pencil down in obvious anger; the point breaks just as there is a KNOCK on the door.

>SCHARFF
>Come!

Richter enters with Kahlil.

>KAHLIL
>You wanted to see me?

There is obvious antagonism between the two men now, Richter turns to leave.

>SCHARFF
>Stay, Richter. I want you to hear this.

He turns to Kahlil; Richter stays; he is obviously ill-at-ease.

>SCHARFF
>His Excellency, the Minister and I are both highly dissatisfied with your performance, Kahlil.

>KAHLIL
>The California mission is - unusual. It probably should never have been attempted. It has been extremely difficult. Extremely - delicate.

                    SCHARFF
          Delicate! It has been handled with stupid-
          ity!
                    (coldly he contemplates the Iraqi major)
          <u>Khalena neke b'saraha</u>, Abu-Ali. Let there be
          no misunderstanding between us.
                    (Scharff glares at the man; he is building
                     himself into a rage.)
          I demand results, Abu-Ali. Immediate re-
          sults. Understood? The Minister is holding
          <u>me</u> responsible! I will hold <u>you</u> responsible.
          Totally responsible. Is <u>that</u> understood?

Kahlil nods, tight-lipped.

                    SCHARFF
          You have failed in everything. Why has the
          pilot not been eliminated? Answer me. Why?

                    KAHLIL
          My instructions from you, yourself, <u>Cedi</u> were
          to avoid undue suspicion. To make certain to
          dispose of the body without the risk of
          discovery. Or to make it look --

                    SCHARFF
          To hell with instruction! Eliminate him.
          Now! <u>However</u> it has to be done.

                    KAHLIL
          He is - with the woman.

                    SCHARFF
          Then you will have to kill them both, will
          you not?

                                                  DISSOLVE TO:

EXT. KILNS - DAY

It is early morning.

INT. KILN - ANGLE ON TOM AND RANDI

It is still dark inside the kiln except for two streaks of light
from the doorway and the high-set window in the back. Randi and
Tom are still sleeping. Randi is sitting against the stone wall,
her head resting against the soot-blackened rocks; Tom is lying
on the ground next to her; his head in her lap; his knees drawn
up under him.

EXT. WOODED HILL ABOVE KILNS - EXTREME CLOSE-UP BOOTS

A man - unidentified - wearing heavy boots is stealthily walking
through the desert underbrush.

EXTREME CLOSE-UP - HAND HOLDING RIFLE as the man walks on.

CLOSE-UP - BOOTS as the man stops briefly - then continues.

INT. KILN - ON RANDI AND TOM

They are still asleep; Tom stirs fitfully...Suddenly there is the SOUND of a helicopter flying low overhead. Tom is instantly awake and alert. Randi, too, is awake - watching the crouching Tom, as the helicopter SOUND draws away into the distance...

EXT. WOODED HILL ABOVE KILN - EXTREME CLOSE-UP - BOOTS

The man is running quickly away - back the way he came.

INT. KILN

Tom crawls to the doorway; cautiously he looks out; then he hurries to the back wall and scampers up the timbers leaning against it, until he can look out; he watches intently.

EXT. HILL BEHIND KILNS - TOM'S POV

Over the crest a row of men, spread out along the ridge, comes slowly searching through the scrub trees and bushes: Paul, Ward, Hays and several rangers.

INT. KILN - TOM AND RANDI

Tom drops to the floor, urgently he runs to Randi; tugs at her; she gets up and they turn to leave the kiln - and stop dead!

TOM AND RANDI'S POV. In the doorway to the kiln stands a mountain lion; stiff-legged, it bares its teeth in a ferocious snarl and crouches, ready to leap at the two people.

ANGLE ON TOM AND RANDI. Randi lets out a little scream, then freezes...Tom at once crouches down, hands on the ground, confronting the mountain lion squarely...The big cat GROWLS - and tenses to leap...Suddenly Tom flings a handful of the charcoal ashes from the floor directly into the face of the SNARLING cat...With a scream of rage and surprise, the creature leaps straight into the air, turns and streaks away...Tom at once grabs Randi and runs with her out through the opening...

DOWN ALONG KILNS. Tom and Randi are running along the kilns away from CAMERA: as they come to the end of the row of stone hives, they are temporarily hidden from view by the searchers on the hilltop. They quickly cross the dirt road and start up the hill slope on the opposite side - OUT OF FRAME.

LONG SHOT - FROM ROAD, BETWEEN TWO KILNS, TO MOUNTAINSIDE. One by one the searchers appear between the pines, slowly walking down toward the kilns. We see Paul, Ward, Hays and several rangers, not including Ranger Gordon.

EXT. SPARSELY VEGETATED HILLSIDE

Tom and Randi come running down the slope; they stop.

TOM AND RANDI'S POV - OLD MINE ORE CONVEYOR RAMP in ruins; the huge wooden ramp looks ready to fall down; the place is deserted.

ON TOM AND RANDI as they begin to run toward the ramp - OUT OF FRAME.

EXT. CONVEYOR RAMP

Tom and Randi appear; they climb up alongside the big ramp; CAMERA - placed on the other side of the ramp - PANS with them as they climb past the sturdy supporting timbers bearing the huge structure. They reach the top of the ramp; Tom crouches down and scans the hills behind them for pursuit; Randi walks on a little - and sits down on the rocky ground, resting.

EXT. CHARCOAL KILNS

In the palm of Paul's hand lies the egg shells from Tom's and Randi's meager meal. Paul turns them over with a finger.

> PAUL
> They've been here all right.

He and ward are examining the shells, in the b.g., Hays and the others are searching.

> WARD
> They seem to be headed for the old mine...

> HAYS
> (calling)
> Captain! Captain Jarman! Over here!

Paul and Ward look up; they start to run toward Hays.

ANGLE ON HAYS standing on a narrow, overgrown trail on the hillside. He is watching the ground; he kneels down and touches it; he looks up as Paul and Ward join him. He points to the ground.

CLOSE SHOT - GROUND. There are tracks of a small vehicle; at the spot where Hays points it appears that the vehicle has been parked. On the ground is a small dark spot. Paul kneels down; he touches the spot - tests the substance on his fingers.

> HAYS
> It's oil, all right.

> PAUL
> (nods)
> Someone parked here.

                              HAYS
                    And it had to be during the night - or early
                    this morning. Or the sun would've dried out
                    the spot.

Paul feels the oil on his fingers; he frowns and looks down
toward the kiln - then back along the trail; he turns to Hays.

                              HAYS
                    Sergeant. Signal the Scouts to pick us up
                    here.

                              HAYS
                    Yes, sir.

He takes a Very Flare Pistol from his belt and fires one flare;
CAMERA PANS UP to follow its soaring flight.

EXT. THE ORE CONVEYOR RAMP

Tom and Randi are resting - sitting near the top of the ramp; in
the far b.g. - over the hills on the horizon - a white flare is
rising high into the air; it is unseen by both.

                                                  DISSOLVE TO:

TOM AND RANDI are resting at the ramp; from the distance, the
SOUND of motors penetrate the quiet; Tom scampers out on the
ramp, crouches there - waiting.

AREA BELOW RAMP - TOM'S POV. In the distance, rounding a huge
rock pile comes a couple of Scouts. CAMERA PANS from them almost
180 degrees to see a jeep and another Scout approaching along the
trail among the abandoned mine ruins.

ANGLE ON RANDI. She looks excited as she HEARS the approaching
vehicles; quickly she bends down and begins to arrange some small
rocks and stones on the ground before her into a pattern.

ANGLE ON TOM ON RAMP as he quickly runs back; he takes Randi's
hand; together they run toward the mine excavations. Randi
glances back at the stones she hastily arranged on the ground.

CLOSE SHOT - STONES ON GROUND. The stones on the ground plainly
spell out:

                         T - O - M

...with a small crude arrow pointing toward the mine area.

MED. SHOT. Tom and Randi are running toward the mine excavation;
they stop; Tom looks down into the mine area below.

TOM'S POV - AREA. The vehicles meet and come to a halt; the men - including Paul, Ward and Hays - get out and look around.

ANGLE ON TOM as he looks around, a cunning expression on his face - first at the many mine adits dotting the hills, then back at the vehicles and the men below...He gets up and pulling Randi along, starts to run <u>back</u> they way they came, doubling back on their tracks - skirting the area where the vehicles are gathered below...

EXT. ORE CONVEYOR RAMP

Several men - including Hays - are climbing up the hill; they reach the spot where Tom and Randi rested only minutes before. Hays is in the lead; he looks around; he walks a few steps toward the excavation - and toward Randi's message on the ground.

CLOSE SHOT - THE STONES ON THE GROUND. The message can be plainly seen.

MED. CLOSE SHOT - HAYS. He is hot; he squints up at the flaming sun; he pulls out his handkerchief and wipes his face; he looks ahead - and walks on toward the excavations.

CLOSE SHOT - THE GROUND - HAYS' FEET. He is taking a couple of steps; unnoticed by him his booted foot kicks at the stone message left by Randi - utterly obliterating it.

LONG SHOT. The rest of the searchers join Hays; they separate; Hays goes off with one of the rangers, CAMERA FOLLOWS. Suddenly Paul's VOICE is he heard in the distance.

                        PAUL (O.S.)
   Sergeant Hays!

Hays starts down the hill.

                            HAYS
   Yes, sir, coming!

MINE AREA. Among the ruins of the mining camp, Paul, Ward and the rangers are gathered around the vehicles. A jeep comes driving up and stops. Ranger Gordon dismounts and joins the group. Paul is distributing a few torches and flashlights to the men; Gordon and Hays join the group.

                            PAUL
   I want every one of those mine tunnels
   searched...And remember - if you find them,
   go easy! Don't rough him up <u>whatever</u> happens. You could kill him.

Ranger Gordon gets a flashlight; he and another ranger start to walk toward the mine area.

TWO SHOT - GORDON, RANGER as they are walking.

                    RANGER
          What happened to you?

                    GORDON
          Damned jeep overheated. Had to use my
          canteen water to cool it down.
                    (motions toward the mine area)
          They holed up in there?

                    RANGER
          Seems like it.

They walk on.

MINING AREA - THE VEHICLES as the men leave the vehicles and fan out into the mining area.

                                        DISSOLVE TO:

EXT. GHOST TOWN (RHYOLITE) - WIDE SHOT - NIGHT

Tom and Randi come walking among the ruins...

CLOSE ANGLE - TOM AND RANDI. They are obviously exhausted; they go - OUT OF FRAME.

SHOT - HUGE RUIN. Tom and Randi climb over the debris; they find a small sheltered spot where they settle down.

CLOSER ANGLE - SHELTERED SPOT. Tom rips off a few withered leaves from a weed. He sniffs them - and throws them away. Randi, watching him, looks dazed from fatigue, thirst and hunger...Tom gets up and starts to move away; resignedly Randi also starts to get up; Tom gently pushes her down; he moves away - stopping to make sure Randi stays; he disappears among the ruins...Randi looks after her husband - too tired to do anything else; she sinks down - exhausted...

                                        CUT TO:

EXT. OUTSKIRTS OF GHOST TOWN - ANGLE ON TOM - NIGHT

He is creeping among the ruins at the outskirts of the deserted town. He looks out over the desert ahead; he sees something.

DESERT CAMPING GROUNDS - TOM'S POV. On the desert near a couple of telephone poles stand a trailer and a car. There are no signs of occupants, but a campfire is smoldering near the trailer.

CLOSE SHOT - RUINS as Tom silently moves out - and disappears.

                                        CUT TO:

EXT. OLD CEMETERY - ANGLE ON TOM - NIGHT

He is making his way among the old tombstones and markers; he crouches down behind one of them and watches.

CUT TO:

EXT. CAMPING GROUNDS - TRAILER AND CAR - TOM'S POV - NIGHT

There is still no sign of life near the trailer, but a dim glow of light can be seen through the curtained windows. In front of the trailer stands a couple of camp chairs; a short distance from the trailer a couple of camping ground garbage cans have been placed along a sort of "squared off" U-shaped wall, a dying campfire glows nearby.

ANGLE ON TOM as he stealthily approaches the cans; cautiously he comes all the way up to them; he begins to fish out various items.

CAMERA REPOSITIONS to see the trailer in b.g. Suddenly the door to the trailer opens, spilling light. A MAN and a WOMAN emerge; she is carrying a full, brown paper bag; they head for the garbage cans and the smoldering fire. Tom instantly crouches out of sight between the garbage cans and the wall.

ANGLE ON TOM crouching behind the cans; his eyes are wild.

WIDER ANGLE. The man stops at the fire and begins to kick sand over the embers; the woman continues toward the garbage cans. She is almost at the cans - when Tom suddenly leaps out from behind them to stand crouched and menacing before the startled woman. She screams. Tom looks ferocious, desperate; he growls deep in his throat; he is defending his precious food from an intruder...Slowly he begins to advance upon the petrified woman; his hands come up before him...The woman lurches back; she drops the brown bag. She screams again; frantically she stumbles back. In the b.g., the man suddenly bends down to the fire; he grabs a heavy stick - glowing ember red at the end - and rushes toward the woman and Tom. As he swings the firebrand through the air, it bursts into flame...Tom is getting ready to leap at the woman.

CLOSE SHOT - TOM. Teeth bared in a vicious snarl, he leaps directly at CAMERA.

WIDER ANGLE. The woman - terror-stricken - reels back - and in this instant the man reaches her; he pushes her violently out of the way to fall to the ground, and thrusts out his flaming torch straight in front of him.

CLOSE SHOT - TOM'S POV. The man is thrusting his blazing firebrand directly at Tom - and CAMERA.

WIDER ANGLE. The flaming firebrand is almost directly in Tom's face; he lets out a howl - and stumbles back. The man swings the fiery torch frantically back and forth in front of him - driving him back, away from the woman on the ground. Tom is slowly retreating from the fire - stumbling backwards, snarling with fear and rage. He bumps into the bag of garbage dropped by the woman; never taking his eyes off the man and his whirling firebrand, he quickly scoops it up...and turns to flee into the dark desert.

CUT TO:

EXT. RUIN SHELTER - NIGHT

CLOSE SHOT - FOOD ON THE GROUND. On the brown bag lies the food leavings picked up by Tom; carrot tops, pieces of melon rinds, celery tops, a bread wrapper with a few slices of stale bread, the empty tin of a canned ham with some fat still left, some wilted lettuce and a pile of chicken bones with quite a bit of meat on them. Two cans of coke with a sip or two and a milk carton half full of sour milk.

ANGLE ON TOM AND RANDI both looking at the food scraps. Then Randi looks up at Tom, her expression one of pride and tenderness. Tom pushes the food toward her; she picks up a melon rind; she looks at it, fighting down her revulsion; she breaks the rind in a couple of pieces.

CLOSE SHOT - MELON RIND IN RANDI'S HAND. Moisture is forming in the breaks. Randi brings the rind to her mouth and sucks the moisture from it; Tom follows her example as CAMERA WIDENS.

CLOSE SHOT - FOOD SCRAPS lying on the ground, with the exception of the two pieces of melon rind. Tom's and Randi's hands come into the PICTURE simultaneously and pick up two more rinds.

DISSOLVE TO:

CLOSE SHOT - THE GROUND - LATER. There are no more food scraps left; only the crumpled up bread wrapper.

ANGLE ON TOM AND RANDI. Randi leans back and runs her fingers through her hair. Tom is watching her. He looks tired and vulnerable. Randi looks earnestly at him, speaking to him, knowing he can't understand what she is saying.

                    RANDI
Tom. I wish I could make you know how I feel. I love you...and I feel so helpless... I wish I could make up for all the times you needed me...for all the times things needed to be said between us...If only I could make you understand...

Tears of emotion well in her eyes. Tom moves to her; with intense curiosity he touches the tears and examines them, moist on his finger - not understanding, but sensing something is wrong, wanting to help. Randi looks at him with great tenderness, her defenses being cast away. Gently she caresses Tom's face. Tom responds to the soft, stroking sensation and in turn caresses her hair, her neck - her shoulders...Randi cups his head in her hands, pulls his face close to hers and kisses him on the eyes and then fully on the mouth. She softly pulls away and slowly opens her blouse and lets it slide down her arms; she opens the zipper on Tom's torn suit and it falls away, exposing his chest; with her hands she caresses him.

Tom responds. For a moment they just stand silent - naked to one another - among the stark ruins; then Randi takes Tom's hand and they come together in a tight embrace - sinking down on the discarded clothing on the ground. And they make love...

                                                                             DISSOLVE TO:

EXT. RANGER HEADQUARTERS - DAY

Several military vehicles and ranger trucks are parked outside the building. A Scout draws up and Colonel Howell gets out and walks briskly toward the building.

INT. RANGER HEADQUARTERS

Gathered in the office are Paul, Ward and Stark. They are grouped around the large map on the wall; their backs to the open door.

                      WARD
          If we don't get them today - I don't see how
          they can survive...It's 120 degrees out
          there.

Paul resolutely turns to Stark.

                      PAUL
          Can we reach the radio stations that serve
          this area?

                      STARK
              (nods)
          By phone.

Howell appears in the open doorway unnoticed by the three men.

                      PAUL
          We'll request them to broadcast an alert. On
          <u>my</u> responsibility! I want every camper,
          every hiker, every damned tourist looking for
          them.

                    HOWELL
          Good day, gentlemen!

The three men all turn toward him, startled. Paul looks at him
with ill-concealed animosity.

                    PAUL
          Colonel Howell! We didn't expect you up
          here.

Howell looks grim; he walks into the room.

                    HOWELL
          I hope my presence won't cramp your style,
          Captain.

                    PAUL
               (stiffly)
          We're planning today's search procedure.

                    HOWELL
          So I heard.
               (angrily)
          Didn't I tell you, Captain, to keep Darby's
          condition confidential until I changed your
          orders?

Paul looks tensely stony; he obviously controls himself only with
difficulty; he makes no reply.

                    HOWELL
          Well?!

                    PAUL
          Yes, sir!

                    HOWELL
          Is that all you have to say?

                    PAUL
          No, sir, it is not! But I'm somewhat under a
          handicap - facing a 'superior' officer!

Howell turns red with controlled anger; he turns to Ward.

                    HOWELL
          That's all, Major Ward.

                    WARD
          Yes, sir.

Howell turns to Stark.

                    HOWELL
          May I have the use of your office?

                              STARK
              Of course.

He and Ward leave. Howell turns back to face Paul; the two men
glare at one another. Howell speaks with ominous calm.

                              HOWELL
              You may speak off the record -- if you have
              anything to say.

                              PAUL
              I do! This entire operation has been ham-
              strung from the start. Mismanaged. By you.
              And - dammit! - I want to know why!

                              HOWELL
              I don't _have_ to give you any reasons for my
              actions - but I did...You _know_ why it has
              been necessary to --

                              PAUL
              Sure. I know. For Tom's own good. Let him
              kill himself out there - for his own damned
              good!

                              HOWELL
              Captain!

                              PAUL
              And now Randi, too...That ought to satisfy
              everybody.

There is a moment's tense silence. Howell glares at Paul; then
he collects himself with a conscious effort.

                              HOWELL
              So you want to make this thing into a circus.
              A goddamned radio show!

                              PAUL
              Oh, hell! That's not what I want and you
              damned well know it. We need help - and _they_
              can give it to us.

Howell controls himself with difficulty.

                              HOWELL
              Every man on the base who knows about Darby
              is rooting for us to get to him. That
              includes you - and _me_. For you it's a simple
              matter. Get everybody out looking! For me
              there are other important considerations...
              There's the safety of Tom himself...

PAUL
We could have figured a way to keep him from harming himself.

HOWELL
...and - primarily - security.

PAUL
Security! What security! Sure I know the F-22 is classified - but there's not one piece of classified hardware left on that damned wreck. It holds no secrets.

HOWELL
But Tom does.

Paul suddenly looks disturbed; he gives Howell a questioning look.

HOWELL
Tom not only flies the F-22 enhancement tests. He's involved in the XM-9 Project as well. And that *is* a top secret project.
                (Paul reacts)
The XM-9 was aboard Tom's plane. He was testing it. At maximum output. First wet run. He was riding a guided missile!

PAUL
        (shaken)
I didn't know.

HOWELL
You had no need to know. Tom did. Tom knew. And may still...But we don't want *everyone* to know. That's why we stuck to routine, dammit! We know foreign powers are aware of the Marcus project and are trying to get any information about it they can. That device took ten years to develop. Unless Tom can tell us exactly *what* went wrong up there - those ten years will have been wiped out in ten seconds.

PAUL
Colonel. There's something you should know.

Howell is aware of Paul's sudden change.

HOWELL
Yes?

PAUL
Until just a moment ago - until you told me about the XM-9 - I didn't put it all together.

Howell is suddenly alert.

HOWELL
What is it?

PAUL
Two things. First - there was the disappearance of Adams. And then - this morning - near a place where Tom and Randi had been holed up for the night, we found an oil stain on the ground. Fresh. Someone had been parked there - shortly before, not one of ours...Who? Why?

Howell frowns.

PAUL
I know it's damned thin, but I do have this gut feeling. Someone <u>outside</u> our own rescue efforts is hunting for Tom!

Howell contemplates him gravely.

HOWELL
You're right. It <u>is</u> thin...

PAUL
I know. It's no neon sign proclaiming: Foreign Intrigue! But is it ever?

HOWELL
It <u>is</u> something to be considered. Perhaps - perhaps <u>they</u> are also aware that Tom is our only hope of saving the Marcus project years of delay. Perhaps they figure - if the desert doesn't kill him, they'll finish the job...

PAUL
We know that yesterday Tom and Randi were at an abandoned mine...

He picks up a key with a large tag on it from the desk and hands it to Howell.

PAUL
Randi left this for us to find near an old tunnel...we checked it...it's the old key to her cabin.

HOWELL
Clever girl.

                    PAUL
          And last night, a camper's report puts them
          at the ghost town...here...

As Paul talks, he is pointing out the spots on the wall map.

                    PAUL
          They're headed for this area here...the black
          desert. And we can make sure they go there
          by keeping that part of the valley clear -
          and sending our choppers in to search behind
          them - herding them.

                    HOWELL
          Why that particular area?

                    PAUL
          I think we have a found a safe way of getting
          him.

                                                  CUT TO:

EXT. NATIONAL GUARD MARSHALLING AREA - DAY

Troops are boarding several trucks and moving out...

EXT. DESERT - HELICOPTERS - VARIOUS SHOTS

They are flying over the desert mountains and the desert, quite low.

EXT. EDWARD AFB - VARIOUS SHOTS

Air Force E.S.T. and security troops are hurriedly boarding trucks...The trucks move out...

EXT. DESERT - HELICOPTER

It is searching the desert floor below...

EXT. FOOTHILLS

A road is running through the hills; on the hillside near the crest two figures can be seen climbing up; it is Paul and Ward; below on the road, two Scouts are parked; an AIRMAN stands leaning against one of them. They reach the crest of the hill; they search the barren countryside before them with their binoculars.

ANGLE ON PAUL sweeping the area before him with his binoculars.

                    PAUL
          Where the hell are they?

BINOCULAR SHOT - PAUL'S POV. The hills are barren and forbidding as Paul's view traverses them.

ANGLE ON PAUL. He lowers his binoculars; he looks up at the sun and wipes his brow; it is already getting hot...Again he starts to search the hills with his binoculars.

BINOCULAR SHOT - PAUL'S POV. Slowly the binocular view passes over the distant hills...Suddenly there is movement. The binoculars stop - and at once return to the spot...Tom and Randi can be seen making their way down the rock-strewn hillside.

                    PAUL (O.S.)
          I got them! Over there! Two o'clock.

The two figures are plainly seen...Suddenly Tom spins around; he clutches his side and falls to the ground. Almost at once a faint CRACK reaches the ears of Paul. Even as he watches - little geysers of dust spurt up close to the supine Tom.

                    PAUL (O.S.)
          My God! He's been shot! Someone's shooting
          at him!

As Randi throws herself over Tom's body, Paul's binoculars whip across the scene to a hillside opposite the location of Tom and Randi. There is a glint of sun-on-metal, a fire flashpoint - another faint CRACK...

THE RIDGE - PAUL, WARD, as they start to scramble down the hill toward the Scouts below. Paul calls:

                    PAUL
          Get to him, Ward! Do what you can for
          him..Inform Howell...

ANGLE ON THE TWO SCOUTS. Paul comes tumbling down the hillside; he leaps into a Scout - and roars off...

EXT. HILLSIDE

Randi is helping Tom crawl behind a rock; he is touching his side uncomprehendingly; his hand comes away wet with blood - but he has obviously only been grazed.

                    RANDI
          Oh, dear God - they are <u>hunting</u> you! Shoot-
          ing at you...Oh dear God...
                    (she looks around frantically)
          Damn you! Goddamn you!...

EXT. FOOTHILLS COMING DOWN TO DRY LAKE

A Scout is racing along the road toward the hills.

CLOSER ANGLE - SCOUT. A grim-faced Paul is careening along.

WIDE SHOT. The Scout is nearing the foothills...Suddenly a dune buggy comes shooting out of a canyon road; the driver sees the approaching Scout and at once veers away - racing out over the dry lake...Paul's Scout pursues.

EXT. THE CHASE - DRY LAKE

As Paul tries to ram and stop the buggy - which is driven by <u>the Artist</u>. The two vehicles roar down the dry lake - sides touching and grating...Suddenly Paul leaps from his Scout into the buggy...Startled, the Artist fights to keep the vehicle under control as Paul's Scout, now driverless, all at once turns over and tumbles end over end in a cloud of dust, to EXPLODE in a huge ball of fire...Suddenly Paul, fighting for control, stomps on the buggy brakes. Taken unprepared, the Artist rams his head against the windshield frame; Paul grabs the wheel and yanks it sharply across - the buggy turns sharply and the Artist flies from the vehicle, hits the ground and, limbs flailing grotesquely, goes tumbling violently to a dead stop...Paul brings the vehicle to a halt; he turns it around and heads back toward the still figure of the Artist.

CLOSER ANGLE. Paul stops the buggy; he dismounts - and walks up to the man sprawled on the cracked dry lake bed. He is dead...

WIDER ANGLE. Two Scouts come racing across the dry lake toward Paul; they reach him - and Ward jumps out.

CLOSER ANGLE - WARD, PAUL. The Scouts can be seen in the b.g.

                    WARD
    We lost them, Paul. They were gone.

                    PAUL
    Then he's alive.

                    WARD
    He's alive.

Suddenly an airman in one of the Scouts holds up a walkie-talkie; he calls:

                    AIRMAN
    Captain!...Sir!

CLOSE SHOT - AIRMAN

                    AIRMAN
    They've spotted them! From the chopper,
    sir...They're headed out on the black
    desert...!

EXT. VOLCANIC ASH FIELD NEAR CRATER - HELICOPTER SHOT - DAY

The black sand of the rolling field stretches to the mountains. A white-yellow bush-weed grows sparsely all over the black expanse, giving the scene an unreal aspect - like a huge negative picture. Two small lone figures are trudging across the black desert. It is Tom and Randi.

ANGLE ON TOM AND RANDI. They are both in a state of exhaustion. Randi valiantly strives to keep up with her husband...

PANNING SHOT. Tom and Randi walk past CAMERA and plod on. CAMERA PANS with them to a REVERSE ANGLE SHOT. As they walk away from CAMERA, we see ahead of them the rim of the crater, and the break in its steep side. Suddenly - faintly from the distance - comes the SOUND of motor vehicles toiling through the sand in low gear. Tom and Randi both look toward the NOISE.

TOM AND RANDI'S POV. In the distance across the volcanic ash field several vehicles formed in a long line slowly converge upon the fleeing man and woman...In one Scout are Ward and Gordon; in another Paul and Hays; in a third Howell and a DRIVER. Other military and ranger vehicles flank them.

ANGLE ON TOM AND RANDI. Tom begins a tortured half-run away from the oncoming vehicles, dragging Randi along.

                      RANDI
    Please, Tom...No more. Please let them get
    to us. Help us...Please...

ANOTHER ANGLE. Tom and Randi are nearing the slope on the outside of the crater; they veer away from the break into the crater bottom. As they do, a couple of ranger trucks can be seen coming slowly on - driving them back on course; a couple of ranger jeeps follow...Tom and Randi veer over to the other side. Again we see a couple of different ranger trucks toiling down upon them. They stop in indecision; they look back toward the Scouts.

TOM AND RANDI'S POV - SCOUTS with Ward, Paul and Howell. The Scouts are now considerably closer; they bear down on Tom and Randi.

ANGLE ON THE OTHER RANGER TRUCKS AND MILITARY VEHICLES also coming toward Tom and Randi.

ON TOM AND RANDI. They look from one group of pursuing vehicles to the other; they are boxed...Suddenly the piercing SOUND of a horn blasts out over the desert; the blaring of the horn is taken up all around them. Tom looks around in panic; they are literally being herded toward the break leading into the crater bottom - into the giant trap - quickly Tom turns and, grabbing Randi, he starts to run to the break.

LONG SHOT - FROM RIM OF CRATER TOWARD INSIDE BREAK SLOPE. Tom and Randi are just starting down the slope into the crater.

ANGLE ON VEHICLES as they arrive at the top of the break and stop. In the center are three Scouts, flanked by two ranger trucks at either end. Slowly the vehicles start down the slope into the crater after Tom and Randi.

ANGLE ON TOM AND RANDI. They have reached the small, almost circular area at the center of the crater; they run out into the little level spot - and stop dead. They look up at the steep walls - stunned. (The laboring of the Scout, jeep and truck motors provide an ominous obligato to the following scenes.)

CLOSE-UP - TOM as he is looking up; he looks trapped - and he is! He begins to look around the crater rim in desperation.

PANNING SHOT - THE CRATER RIM - TOM'S POV. 100 feet above towers the rim of the crater; CAMERA PANS along the entire circle; the crater walls are unscalable, except in one place; the break slope. CAMERA PANS all the way to the slope; the Scouts, jeeps and trucks are slowly driving down toward Tom and Randi.

ANGLE - FROM CRATER RIM. Below in the crater bottom Tom and Randi scurry across the sand like tiny ants; on the slope the vehicles are driving down.

ON TOM AND RANDI. Like a caged animal, Tom turns to look around; there is no way out - and the NOISY monsters move toward him, finally - half-dragging Randi along - he turns to run away from the pursuing creatures toward the towering crater wall - bent on doing the impossible - if it costs them their lives.

ANGLE ON PAUL IN SCOUT. He sees that Tom is trying to scale the crater wall; he motions for Hays to stop; he stands up - and holds a flare pistol into the air.

SHOT - ACROSS SCOUT IN F.G. TO CRATER BOTTOM AND RIM. Paul is standing in the Scout; below in the crater, Tom and Randi are running for the far wall. Paul fires a flare into the air. CAMERA PANS UP to catch it - and to see the crater rim. Suddenly - all along the rim, a ring of black smoke columns spring into being - rising toward the sky, and from every point a blazing, smoking clump of kerosene-soaked brush tumbles over the edge and plunges down - trailing a long tail of sparks and smoke.

ANGLE ON RANGER ON THE RIM setting a clump of brush afire and pushing it over the rim. The CRACKLING of the fire is loud.

ANGLE ON NATIONAL GUARDSMEN as they are kicking smoking, burning bushweeds over the rim.

ANGLE ON WRANGLERS, RANGERS, NATIONAL GUARD TROOPS AND AIRMEN as they throw down blazing tumbleweeds, and push flaming brush clumps over the side.

ANGLE FROM BREAK SLOPE TOWARD OPPOSITE CRATER WALL. All along the inside crater wall, blazing, CRACKLING, smoking clumps of brush are tumbling down toward the crater bottom.

ANGLE ON TOM AND RANDI. They stand rooted to the spot with fear and shock; both of them look horror-stricken. To Tom - like to any other wild animal - the sight of flaming brush is terrifying!

WIDER ANGLE. The burning firebrands come tumbling down to form a ring of smoking, CRACKLING fire around the two panic-ridden people...The vehicles have almost reached the crater bottom. Tom is looking around in terrified uncertainty. Randi has reached her limit of endurance; she sinks to the ground...Just as Ward's Scout is about to turn; the wheels spin in the volcanic ash as the vehicle gets stuck. Paul's Scout reaches the crater bottom and starts toward Tom and Randi; the trucks take up blocking positions; Howell's Scout follows Paul...Tom is at his wits end; his tortured mind can stand no more; he suddenly runs toward the ring of flaming brush; stops in terror.

ANGLE ACROSS RANDI TO TOM. Randi is lying on the ground; in the b.g. Tom gathers all his courage - and makes a dash through the blazing desert brush.

ANGLE ON TOM racing through the smoke and flames of the blazing brush; his face is wild with terror. He crosses the fire ring; he runs on a few steps - then as if suddenly realizing that his woman is not with him, he stops and looks back.

ANGLE - TOM'S POV. The flames leap between him and Randi, the vehicles are approaching her. Randi raises herself up; looks beseechingly toward Tom; holds out a hand for him - then sinks down again and just lifts her head.

ANGLE ON TOM. Terror still tortures his face - but another stronger emotion is gradually turning it into grim determination; absentmindedly his hand strays to touch the blood-caked wound on the crown of his head.

WIDER ANGLE as Randi sinks down in utter despair; Paul is almost at her side. Tom snarls in rage; he leaps <u>back</u> through the flaming brush; he races to Randi's side; at the same time, Paul has jumped from the Scout and run to the girl. With a fierce animal SOUND - half-growl, half-scream - Tom throws himself at Paul.

THE FIGHT. Tom fights viciously, not like a human being - but like an enraged, wild animal. He snarls, he bites, he scratches, he kicks. Howell and Hays join the furious battle, while Ward stands by with a hypodermic and rangers ring the fighters. Randi looks on in horror...Air Force personnel begin to battle the flames; others ring the men struggling with Tom...The men fight with a great handicap; they cannot hurt Tom, only try to subdue him. But no restrictions hamper Tom and he inflicts a lot of damage...Howell's face is raked by Tom's nails - as the officer deliberately stays from striking him; Paul is scratched and beaten, as he tries to pin Tom's arms without hurting him, and Hays' arm is gashed by Tom's teeth...From one of the vehicles
CONTINUED:

CONTINUED:

Ranger Gordon runs toward the fight; he holds something concealed against his body. A slight stumble reveals what it is - a steel-blue tire iron! But it is unnoticed by anyone else...Gordon runs to the group of struggling men - he lifts his lethal weapon, waiting for an opportunity to crash it down on Tom's head...With horror Randi sees it. She leaps on Gordon's back, clawing at him...The deadly tire iron flies from the man's hand as he tries to free himself from Randi's infuriated attack - but he is bloodied before Stark and a couple of rangers are able to pull her off. Stark stares at Gordon.

                   STARK
     Hold on to the bastard!

Two rangers grab Gordon. At last Tom is defeated. The men manage to pin his arms and legs; Ward at once shoots the hypo into his arm - and Tom is gently lowered to the sandy ground - barely conscious...

WIDE ANGLE. Tom is quiet and still - but the scene around him is one of NOISE, and hectic activity. Randi runs to her husband; she cradles his head in her arms. Ward is making a cursory examination; he nods with satisfaction - Tom will be okay...From one of the Scouts an airman calls to Howell, who hurries over.

ANGLE ON SCOUT as Howell listens and talks on the radio.

ANGLE ON GROUP WITH TOM. Gordon is nearby. Paul stands protectively over Randi and Tom. In the b.g., a USAF helicopter is landing on the crater bottom, two MEDICS at once leap out and hurry toward the group, carrying a stretcher...Paul turns to Gordon - as Howell comes striding over. He glares at the man.

                   PAUL
     You bastard. What the hell were you going to
     do?

Howell joins them.

                   HOWELL
     I don't know who you are, mister. But I'll
     sure as hell find out!...They found the <u>real</u>
     Gordon. Dead. In the trunk of his own
     car...

He snaps his head at the rangers, and they lead Gordon off. Paul turns back to Tom and Randi.

CLOSER ANGLE. Paul bends down to Randi; she looks at him.

                   PAUL
     He'll be okay, Randi. He'll be okay now.

She nods; she looks down at her husband; she speaks softly.

> RANDI
> We'll both be - okay...

She looks back up at Paul with radiant eyes.

WIDER ANGLE. The chopper medics come hurrying up to Tom carrying a stretcher; two other medics arrive with a second stretcher. Tom and Randi are placed on the stretchers; they do not take their eyes from one another, although Tom is fighting to remain conscious. Randi reaches out her arm to him. The medics carry off the two stretchers together and load them on the helicopter. CAMERA (HELICOPTER) PULLS UP to see the entire crater floor; the circle of burning brush; the vehicles; the men - the full scene of hurried activity...and still FURTHER UP to see the whole Ubehebe Crater, as the tiny vehicles begin to labor their way up and out of the crater trap.

> DISSOLVE TO:

EXT. HOSPITAL - EDWARDS AIR FORCE BASE - ESTABLISHING - DAY

INT. HOSPITAL CORRIDOR

Randi, Paul and Trafford are standing outside a hospital room talking in subdued voices.

> PAUL
> There were two of them, Randi. Some guy posing as an artist - and the phony ranger, Gordon.

The door to the room opens and Howell and Marcus come out; Marcus is beaming.

> TRAFFORD
> Did you get what you wanted, Doctor Marcus?

> MARCUS
> Yes. Thank you. Indeed. Major Darby was most helpful.

> PAUL
> Was he able to pinpoint what went wrong?

> TRAFFORD
> Was it sabotage?

> MARCUS
> No-no-no! As a matter of fact, he --

> HOWELL
> I think we'd better let Doctor Marcus get to work.

                    MARCUS
        Yes. Ah - yes, of course.

He leaves.

                    RANDI
        Is it my turn now?

                    TRAFFORD
        Of course. Go on in.

Randi starts for the door to the hospital room.

INT. HOSPITAL ROOM

Tom is half-sitting up in bed; his head is bandaged and he is browned by the sun. He smiles broadly as Randi enters.

                    TOM
        Hi, honey.

                    RANDI
        Hi, yourself.

She walks over and sits on the edge of the bed; for a moment they sit in silence - together.

                    TOM
        Randi. What - what really went down? I have
        to know.

Randi bites her lip; she does not answer.

                    TOM
        I don't remember a damned thing - from the
        moment I hit the ground like a sack of bricks
        - until I woke up here, smelling of disin-
        fectant and wearing this turban.

                    RANDI
        You look cute in it.

                    TOM
        What did happen, Randi?

                    RANDI
        They - they told me not to discuss it with
        you. Not yet...

                    TOM
        I want to know.

                    RANDI
        You were - running.

                                    TOM
                    Running?

                                    RANDI
                    Yes. Running away. From everyone. From the
                    fears - from the demons that existed only in
                    your own mind. I guess - we - we all do
                    that. Sometimes.

He takes her hand.

                                    TOM
                    I'm back, Rand.

                                    RANDI
                    I am - too...

Paul enters.

                                    PAUL
                    Hey! You're famous, old cock!

He tosses a newspaper on the bed. Tom picks it up. On the front page is a photograph of him standing before an F-22 Eagle. The headline reads:

               DOWNED PILOT RESCUED IN DEATH VALLEY

Tom throws the paper on the floor; he looks at Randi.

                                    TOM
                    I've got better things to do than being
                    famous...

CAMERA MOVES TO PAPER. Below-fold on the front page is another headline:

                        NEW SADDAM HUSSEIN PURGE
                     TOP FORMER NAZI ADVISOR EXECUTED

                                                        FADE OUT.

                                <u>THE END</u>

Bear Manor Media

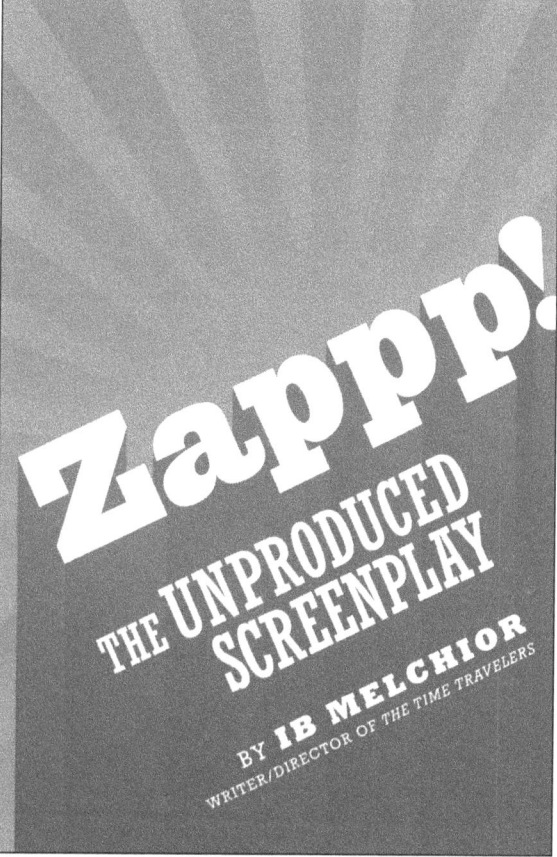

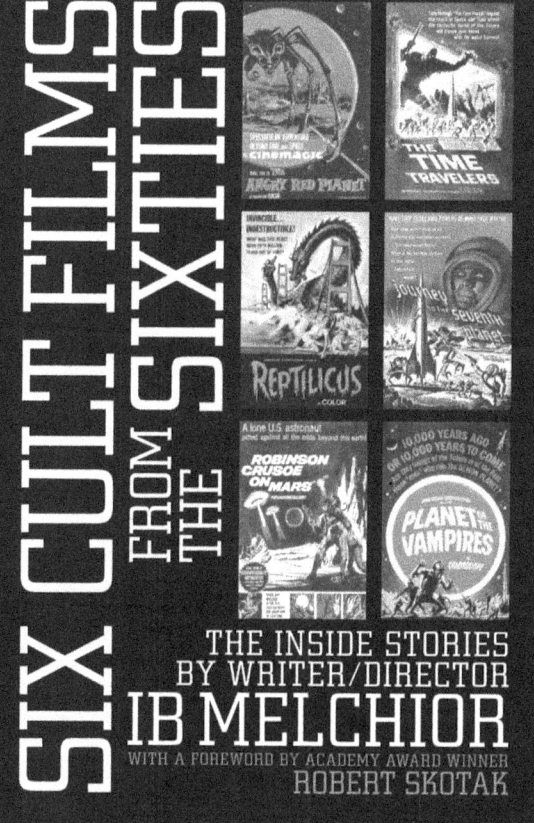

Classic Cinema.
Timeless TV.
Retro Radio.

WWW.BEARMANORMEDIA.COM

www.ingramcontent.com/pod-product-compliance
Lightning Source LLC
Chambersburg PA
CBHW080406170426
43193CB00016B/2824